Temporary Shelter:

An Art Installation About Homeless New Yorkers

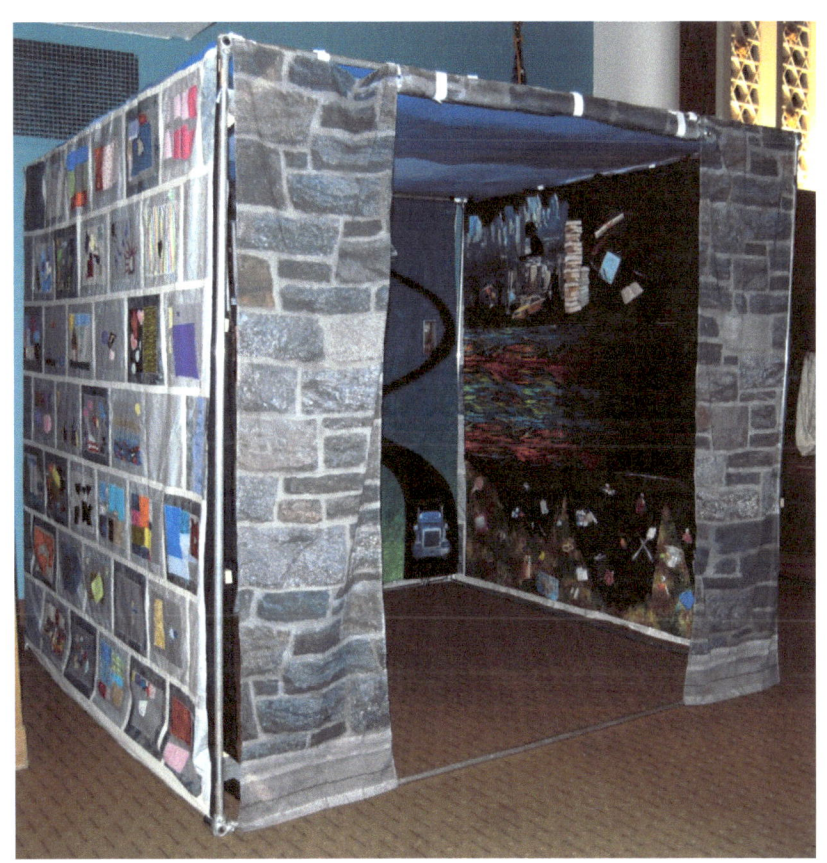

Heather G. Stoltz

CONTENTS

ACKNOWLEDGMENTS

I would never have been able to complete this project without the love and support from my family. To my parents, Brenda and Mel Stoltz, thank you for always believing in me, teaching me to follow my dreams, and encouraging me to pursue my passion. To my husband, Geoff Mitelman, your belief in my vision made me see it was possible to turn this project into reality, and your patience and understanding throughout the creative process, even when it took over our apartment, was invaluable.

A special thank you to the houses of worship who hosted *Temporary Shelter* for its launch tour in New York City: The Church of the Holy Trinity, The Church of St. Francis Xavier, Congregation Shaare Zedek, The Sixth Street Community Synagogue, and Stephen Wise Free Synagogue. The project would also have been impossible without the help of the wonderful volunteers in the Faith-Based Emergency Shelter Network, the Department of Homeless Services, the friends who helped me schlep the piece from one venue to the next, and all of the project's supporters: Pat Adams, Marjorie Berman, Robin Bodner, Jackie Chorney, Debra Nussbaum Cohen, Diane Cooper, Jeanne Drury, Muriel Finkelstein, Marilyn Fishbone, Eric Hamerman, Marisa Harford, Richard Harding, Susan Hill, Miriam (Katz) Holtzman, Laura Hoyt, Pam Johnson, Rabbi Beth Kalisch, Marvin & Barbara Katz, Paula Kaufman, Rochelle Lauer, Lower Manhattan Cultural Council, Benjamin Maron, Faith Miller, Bonnie & Alan Mitelman, Geoffrey Mitelman, Michael Mitelman, Diane Moyer, New York City Department of Cultural Affairs, Carol Kaufman Newman, Helaine & Michael Schlar, Alicia Seiger, Joe & Randee Seiger, Leah Staub, David Strauss, Brenda & Melvin Stoltz, Jennifer & Michael Stoltz, Anne Turner, Bob and Sandy Weiner, Alex, Marika and Cole Wissink, Karen Wojciechowski, Rabbi Julie Wolkoff, Asif Zamir, and Barry Zaret.

Temporary Shelter:
An Art Installation About Homeless New Yorkers

Like so many New Yorkers, I pass homeless people on the street every day and I wonder about them. Who are they? Where are their families? What are their stories? Over the last two years, I had the opportunity to listen to the stories of homeless New Yorkers as I sought to transform their stories into the fiber art installation, *Temporary Shelter*.

This project began in 2008, when I started working as the Community Service Coordinator for the Stephen Wise Free Synagogue (SWFS) in New York City, and spent a lot of time with the residents of their men's shelter. It was there that I learned about New York's Faith-Based Emergency Shelter Network, a network of approximately 100 churches and synagogues in New York City that house volunteer-run homeless shelters. Working with and learning from these incredible lay leaders and spending time with the guests at the SWFS shelter inspired me to tell their stories in the best way I know how – through my art.

I started my interviews at the SWFS shelter, where I already had a relationship with both the coordinators, Ania and Arthur Yorinks, as well as some of the shelter guests. From there, I traveled to two other faith-based shelters in the City: The Church of the Holy Trinity and B'nai Jeshurun. While some of the shelter guests were reluctant to share their stories with me, those who did were completely open about their experiences, and I was humbled by their trust in me.

To hear the stories of another generation, I also spent some time with homeless children. The wonderful people at the Department of Homeless Services put me in touch with recreation teachers at nine family shelters in the City. In each of those shelters, I ran a workshop with the students, helping each child create a small fiber art piece that expressed their feelings about living in the shelter.

To create an art piece embodying these stories, I decided to create a free-standing structure reminiscent of a *sukkah*, a temporary hut constructed for use during the week-long Jewish festival of *Sukkot*. The inside walls of this shelter are made from the stories of the homeless individuals from the faith-based shelters and the outside walls consist of the artwork created by the children in the family shelters. By hanging these stories on the walls of the *sukkah*, the *ushpizin* (exalted guests) who are usually our Biblical ancestors are instead the homeless men, women, and children of our City.

There were two Jewish texts that truly guided the creation of this piece. Sefer Hasidim (a Jewish legal text from the 12th Century) teaches us that "If a community lacks a place of worship and a shelter for the poor, it is first obligated to build a shelter for the poor." And in Vayikra Rabbah 34:1 (a book of *midrashim*, homiletic commentaries, on the book of Leviticus), we learn that "Rabbi Yonah said: The verse does not say 'Happy is the one who gives to a poor person' rather, it says: 'Happy is the one who considers a poor person' (Psalms 41:2). Therefore, you must consider how best to benefit such a person."

I was struck by the directive to build a home for the poor before a house of worship and wanted to create a piece that would resemble a permanent structure. All of the children's art was created using grey fabric as the background and they were pieced together to look like stones when seen from a distance. This feeling is enhanced by the front panels of the piece, which are images of stones from a synagogue façade printed on sheer fabric. A closer inspection of the piece, however, reveals its temporary nature with fabric walls and a sheer roof, reminding us that although we have built shelters for our poor, we do not yet have a permanent solution to the problem of homelessness.

Through the conversations at the shelters, I was also constantly reminded of the vast differences among the people living side by side. Each individual had a unique story that brought him or her to the shelter and each person had different needs. Since the nine inside panels tell nine distinct stories, the viewer is asked to consider them as individuals as Rabbi Yonah instructs, giving attention to one at a time. And although each child started with the same grey background, the art they created reflected their personal journeys.

The first section of this book describes the inside panels in detail, explaining the stories of nine individuals I interviewed in the faith-based shelters. And the second section shows all the children's work, along with selected stories. I hope that as you read through the stories and see the art about these incredible individuals, you will be inspired to more carefully consider the homeless in your city.

Heather G. Stoltz, 2011

INSIDE PANELS:
STORIES FROM NEW YORK'S FAITH-BASED SHELTERS

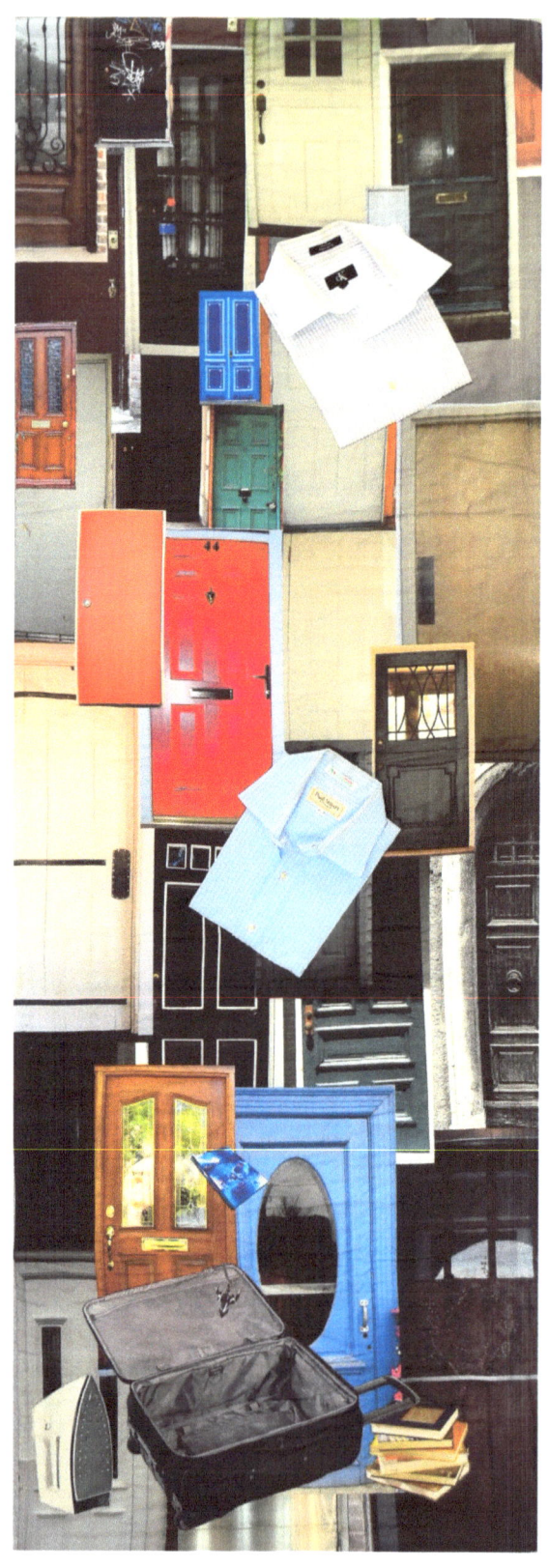

JOE*

Joe lost his job, got divorced, and then found that he could no longer make ends meet. A proud, hard-working man, he didn't want to ask others for help, but could think of no other option. Unfortunately, it was then that he found out that the people he "thought would be there in hard times, weren't." With no family or friends willing to offer a helping hand, he entered the New York shelter system and gained a spot at one of the city's faith-based shelters.

In the shelter system, guests are allowed only one small suitcase. Nothing can be left at the shelter site during the day, so they have to bring it with them wherever they go. How do you put your life in one bag? In his small bag, Joe carefully folded his button down shirts and pants. An avid reader, he also made sure to keep some of his favorite books with him. And of course, he also brought along the necklace given to him by his 9-year-old daughter, that he hasn't taken off since she gave it to him.

Joe settled in at the shelter. Very concerned with maintaining a tidy appearance, he ironed his shirts each morning, encouraging the other shelter guests to do the same. And he found a way to keep up with the latest books, devouring spiritual books that help him keep things in perspective.

But before long, the shelter system also let Joe down. Once he found a job as a security officer and janitor, he was unable to make it to his appointments at the drop-in center. Failure to make the appointments took away his spot at the shelter. Suddenly, he had to start over with the process of regaining one of those precious spots.

It was then that a door was finally opened to him. The shelter coordinator asked Joe to be a permanent volunteer at the shelter. In that role, he helps set up for the evening, checks the guests in as they arrive, and sleeps in the shelter with any other overnight volunteers. And just like the guests and other volunteers, he leaves early in the morning and returns again in the evening.

In order to reflect the feeling of nowhere to go and no one to help, the background of the art piece is made up of many closed doors. Depicted in front of those doors are the few possessions he took with him into the shelter: a few pressed shirts falling into an open suitcase next to a stack of books and an iron. Hanging carefully on the edge of the suitcase is the necklace from his daughter (see detail image on right), a reminder of her unfailing love and his responsibility to her.

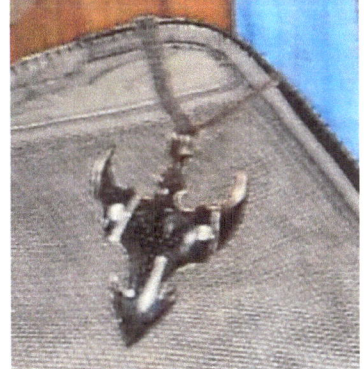

*At his request, Joe's name has been changed.

STEVEN

Steven grew up on the streets of New Jersey. With his mother "running the streets" and his father having died at a young age, he and his three sisters were raised by his grandmother. In sixth grade, he dropped out of school and by the age of 13, was getting high with his friends. Gradually, this led to a life of petty crime and hard drugs.

He was sent to a training school for boys, but fell in with a similar crowd there. In and out of jail throughout his life, Steven finally realized at the age of 42 that this is not what he wanted from life.

"Drugs will destroy your body – mentally and physically," he said. "My goal is to become a decent human being for myself and the Lord; to love myself and not hurt myself." To accomplish this, he entered a 12-step program as well as programs for behavior modification and relapse prevention. He is also learning the plumbing trade and writes poetry that reflects his new outlook on life.

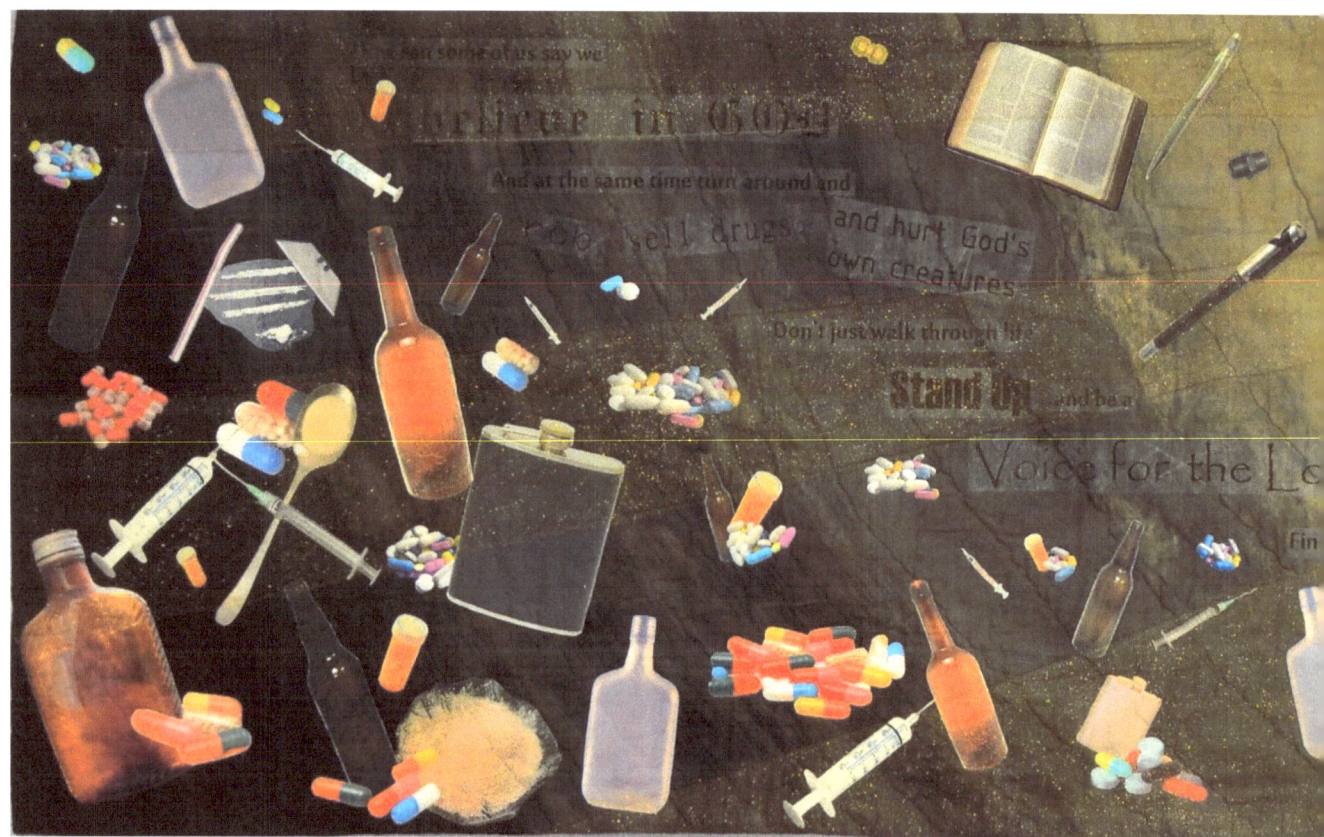

This piece shows Steven's journey from the darkness of drugs to the light of religion, poetry and a career as a plumber. The background is hand-painted and the words from two of his poems were added to the piece by Transfer Artist Paper®.

The first poem, which speaks about his belief in God and the need to do the right thing, acts as a divider between his two lives. The second, a poem he wrote for his mother about believing in yourself, pours out of an open journal toward the light of his new life. In spite of his childhood experiences and having called his grandmother "Mom" and his mother by her first name, Steven's poem reassured his mother to "never ever be afraid to defend your decisions regardless." The rays of light, created by layers of sheer fabric over the images and text, enhance the movement toward Steven's new outlook and new life.

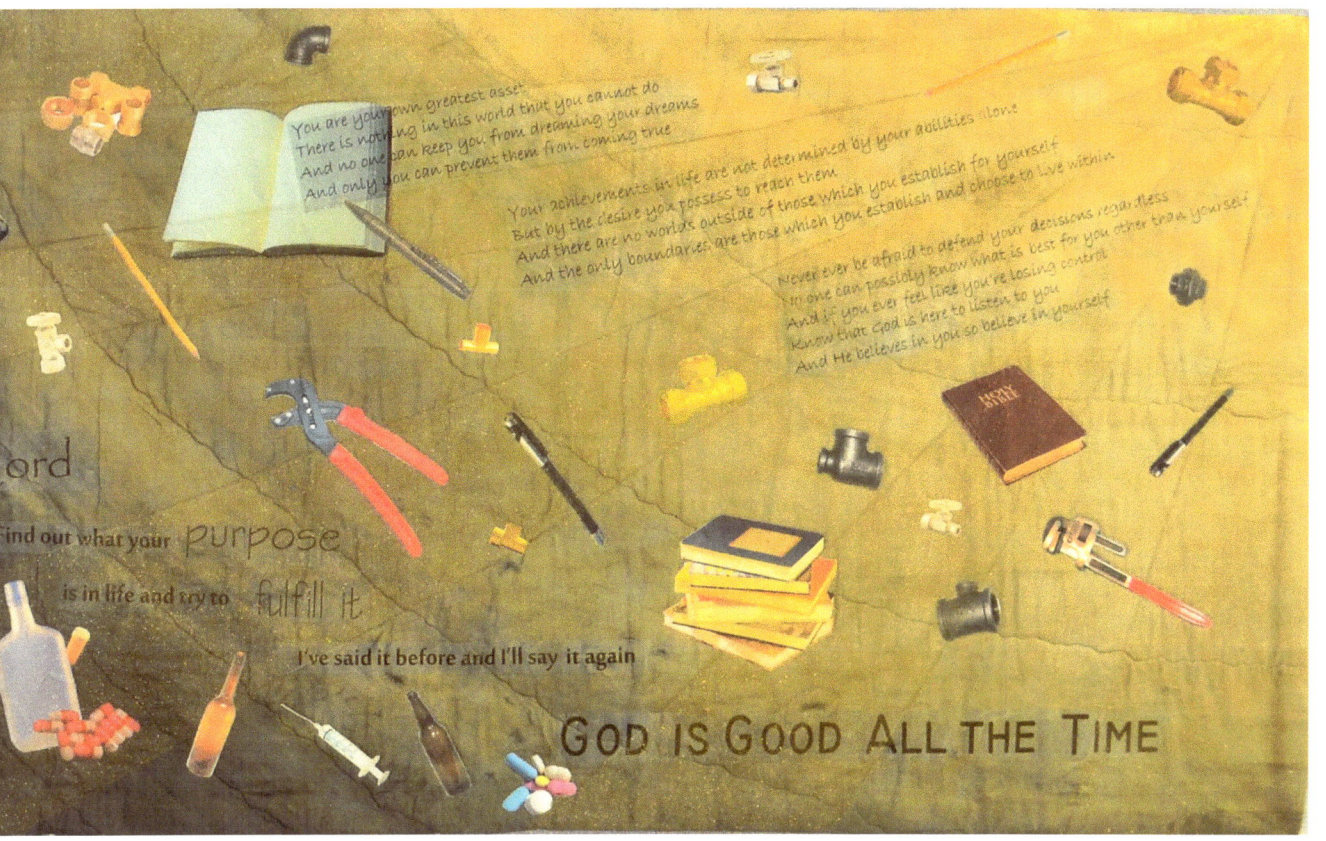

MIRIAM

75-year-old Miriam has held onto her spunk and fight during her year and a half in the New York shelter system. This feisty woman, a passionate advocate for elders and the environment, found herself out on the streets after losing her partner and her home. Ten years in a dedicated relationship with her partner left her no rights to their apartment when her partner passed away following a long illness. When things were at their worst – when the person she loved most in this world was gone and she had nowhere to live and no one to turn to – she had two options: "eat all the bon-bons in the world or fight." She chose to fight.

As a former deacon of her church, she feels that "if there is a higher power, you need to take the second option; otherwise it's a slap in His/Her face." And fight she does. Before receiving a bed in one of the City's faith-based shelters, she advocated for the women in the drop-in center, working to get more women placed in shelter beds. She met many other homeless individuals in these centers and spoke to them about the possibility of creating a book or program that spoke to the "many faces of homelessness." And she continues to work on her website for seniors which provides them the resources needed to advocate for themselves while giving back through volunteer work.

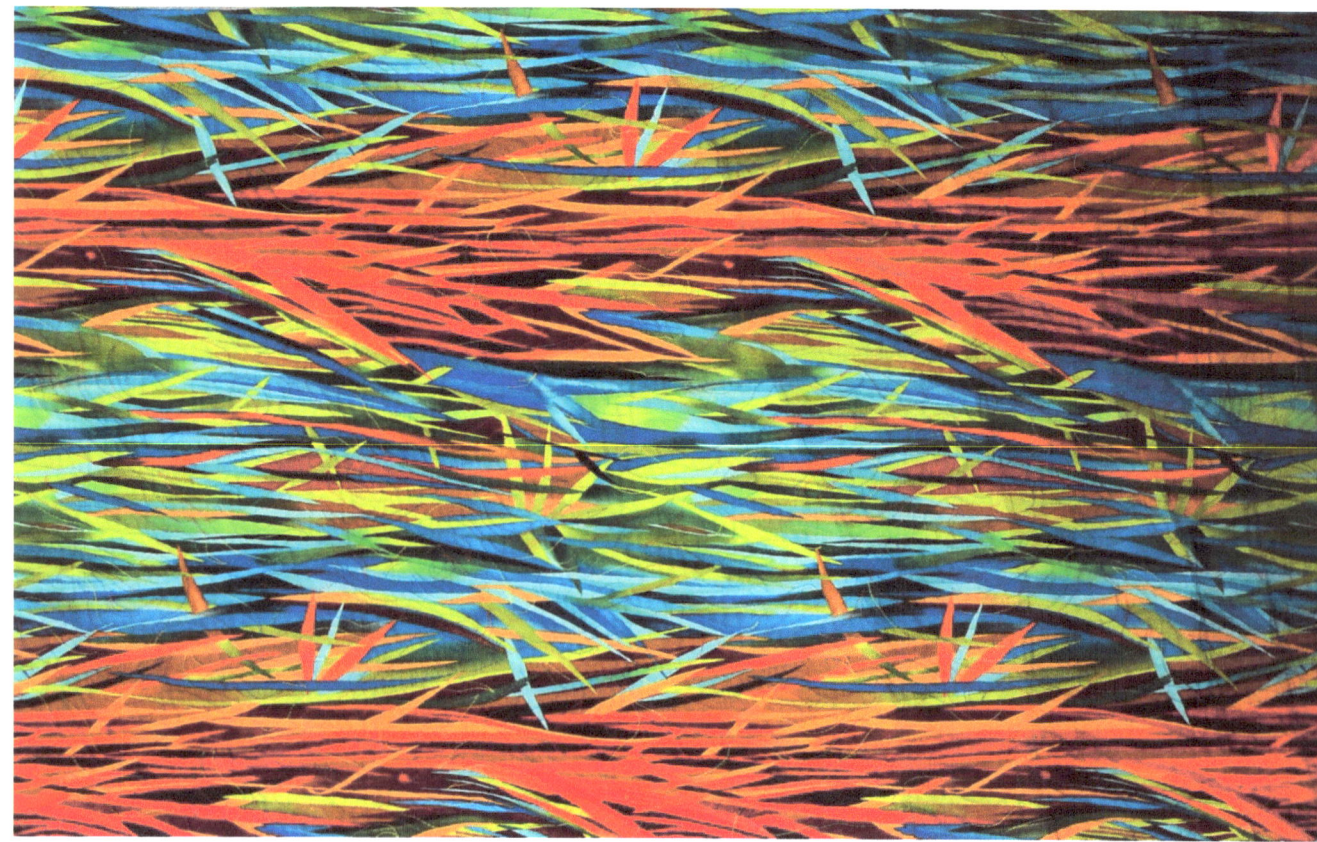

Although she is a fighter, Miriam knows that she can't live in the shelter forever. She has been in the hospital twice in the last fourteen months and knows that this lifestyle is detrimental to her health. She is hoping that the City will soon place her in subsidized housing so she can return to her independent life and advocacy work.

The background of this piece shows her vibrancy and depth while the layers of black tulle show the darkness that she battled through the loss of her partner and home. Although those were dark and difficult times, her brightness shows through even the deepest layers of fabric and, as the piece moves to the right, the darkness decreases as she starts to slowly emerge from that sorrow as she moves forward with her life – trying to get back to a place of her own so she can better help others.

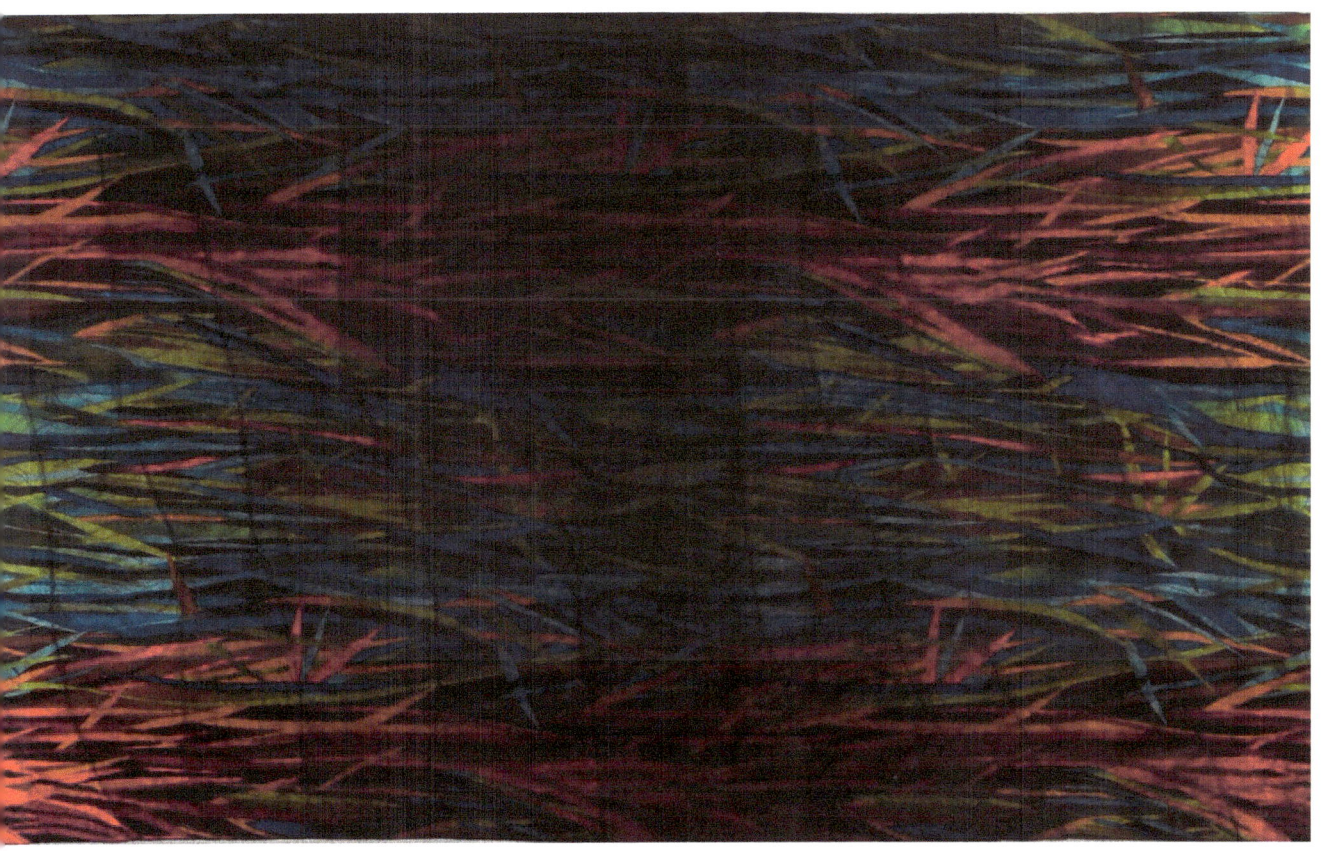

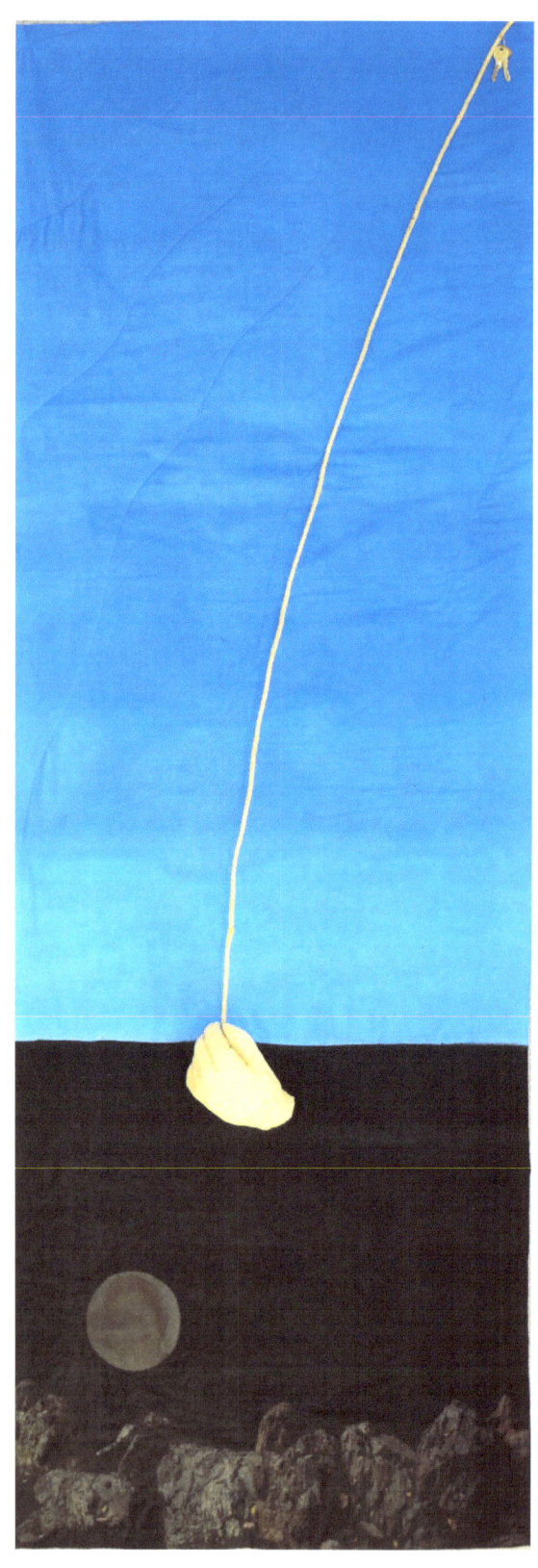

ROGER*

As Roger spoke about the story of his life, the layers of sadness that made up his past and the determination he had to continue his slow journey to a better life were striking. When he was born, his mother was unable to take care of him and his twin brother. His grandmother took care of him and his brother was brought up by their aunt. When he was 2, his father, a drug dealer who had been in and out of jail, took his own life. Over the years, he and his brother got together at family gatherings once or twice a month, but it was his grandmother who raised him – "teaching [him] to sew, cook, and treat women well."

On Valentine's Day when he was 15 years old, his grandmother encouraged him to go visit his mother with whom he had had a difficult relationship. After an argument with his mother, he returned home to find his grandmother in bed, no longer breathing. He held her for the final moments of her life and after that, his life was forever changed.

From the age of 16, he was living on his own. One day, Roger was raped by three men and started taking drugs to block out the memory. Though he tried many times to stop over the years, he continuously slipped back into his old ways.

Now, at the age of 42, Roger is taking control of his life. He decided that he could no longer hide behind drugs and needed to face reality. He has been drug-free for over a year. And although he always worked odd jobs, he is now proud to have a career as a security guard. Even better, he received a housing voucher and was hoping to move out of the shelter soon. The thing he was most proud of was the fact that his 17-year-old son was now back in his life. After 15 years without contact, and after everything Roger did to himself, he was touched that his son still wanted to be part of his life.

The black swirling ocean with black rocks at the bottom symbolizes the sorrow and pain of Roger's past with just one bubble of happiness representing his grandmother and the life they had together. (There is a faint image of the artist's grandmother in the bubble.) Roger's hand emerges from the depths and clings to the rope that he is climbing to his new life. At the top of the rope are keys just like those he will use to enter his new apartment and his new life.

*At his request, Roger's name has been changed.

HEATHER

Heather moved to New York in 2001 with $300 and a dream. And she made that dream a reality. She found a great job as a copy editor at Harper Collins that she enjoyed, and it provided her with an income that allowed her to truly live the Upper East Side life. After two years at the job, however, Heather decided to go back to school for an additional degree in English.

When she graduated in 2008, the economy wasn't what it was when she entered. Direct loans to students were no longer available and there were no jobs to be had. Three years later, she has still not found a position with any reliable income and is living in a faith-based shelter until she can make it on her own again. Her parents (who are retired and living in Georgia) are helping as much as they can and would welcome her back into their home at any time, but Heather is determined to make it on her own. At 37, she doesn't want to be relying on her parents and wants to stay in the city that she has grown to love.

The left side of the piece tells the story of Heather's successful New York life. The city skyline is a backdrop for the silhouettes that show her hard at work at the computer, partying with friends, and shopping. The black background is covered with a gold tulle so the night sky sparkles and the pavement at the bottom of the piece also has a shine to it.

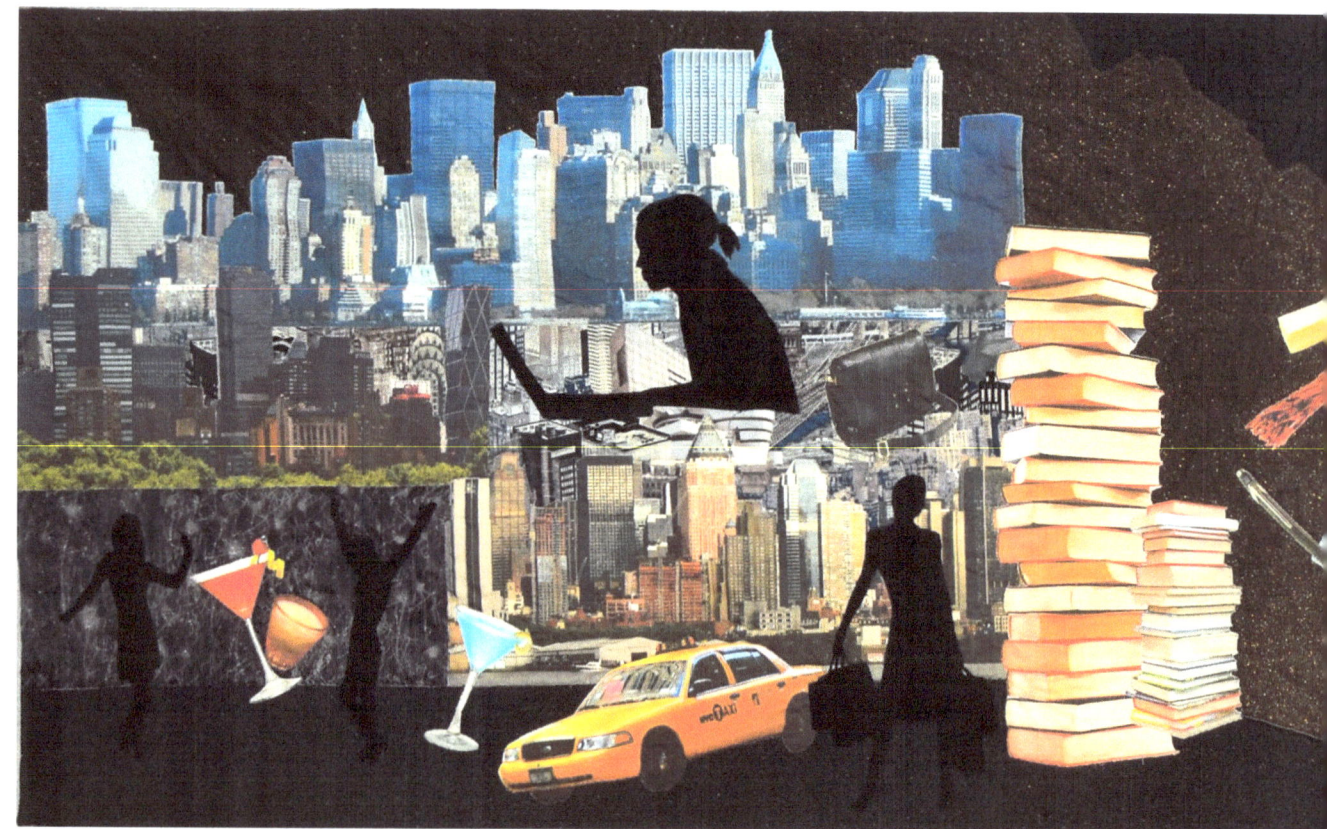

In the next section, the skyscrapers are replaced by stacks of books as she delves into her studies. And once she receives her graduation cap and diploma, the golden backdrop comes to an abrupt end leaving only darkness quilted with free motion zig-zag. Buried in this chaos, however, is a door with an exit sign – a door that is always available to her if she chooses to return to the comfort of her parents' home.

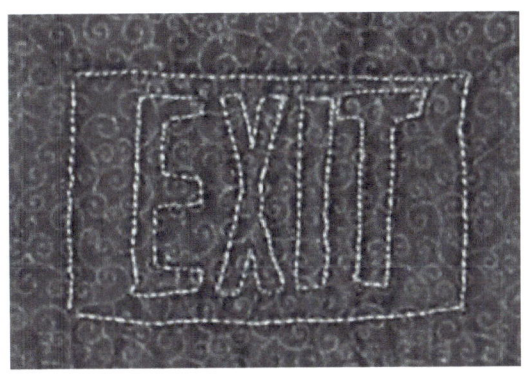

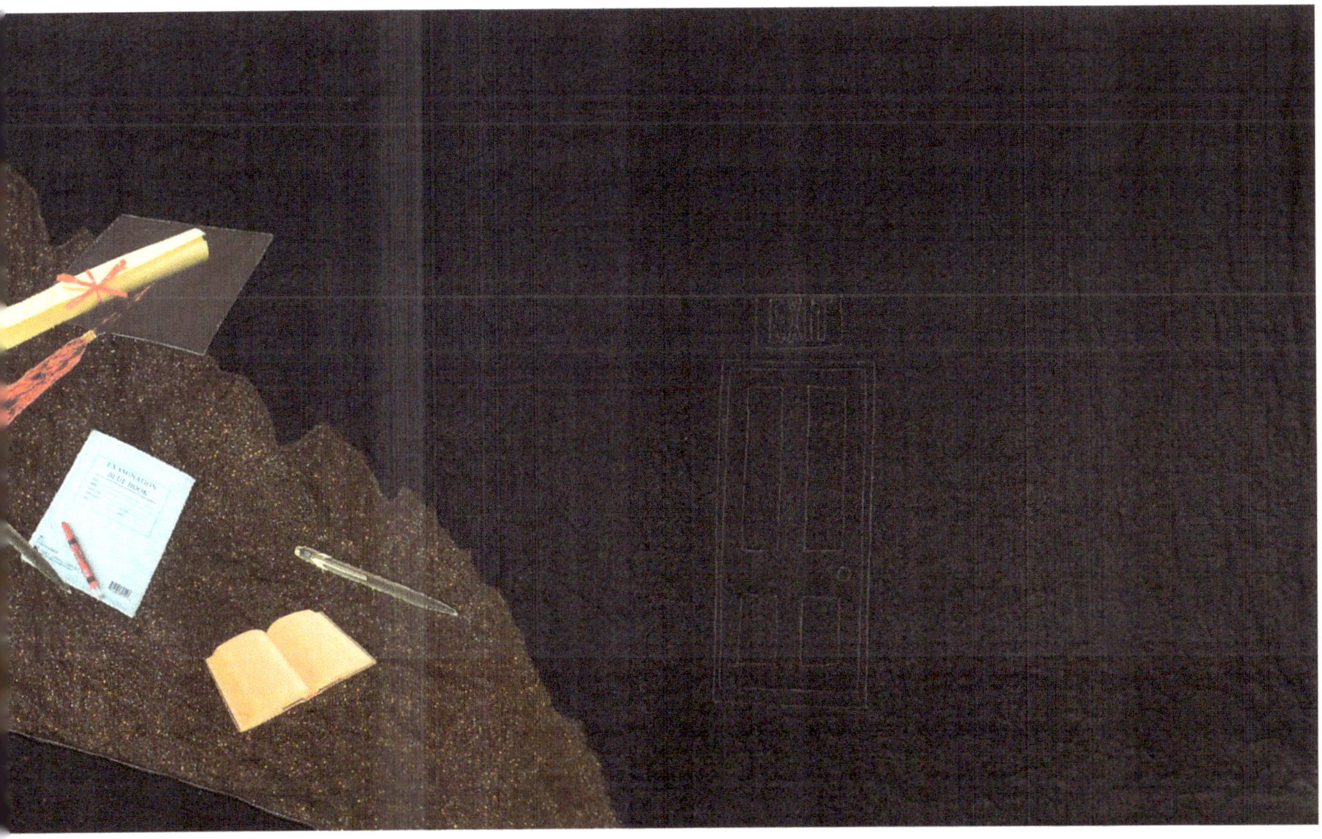

TED*

Ted's life has been a series of ups and downs, so this piece is a timeline of his story. The piece graphs his life from a happy childhood through troubled teen years, a failed marriage and a fight to get clean. Images relating to his story accompany his words, which are written in silver gel pen. The drugs and other challenges that have kept him down are shown on the black fabric in the lows of his life. And the moments in his life that have brought him joy and kept him going are shown below in the thriving green vines that continue to grow from the bottom in spite of the darkness.

Ted had a wonderful childhood, growing up with his 3 sisters in the Bronx. When he was just ten years old, however, his father left for work and never returned. His mother worked two jobs to make ends meet and, at thirteen, Ted started working at his uncle's grocery store. In junior high and high school, he met the wrong crowd and started drinking and smoking marijuana. Soon after, he dropped out of high school and started experimenting with stronger drugs.

In 1968, his girlfriend got pregnant and they married in 1971. At that time, Ted was working in a cancer research hospital, enjoying the work that supported his family. When the hospital was closed, he was transferred to the burn unit of a different hospital.

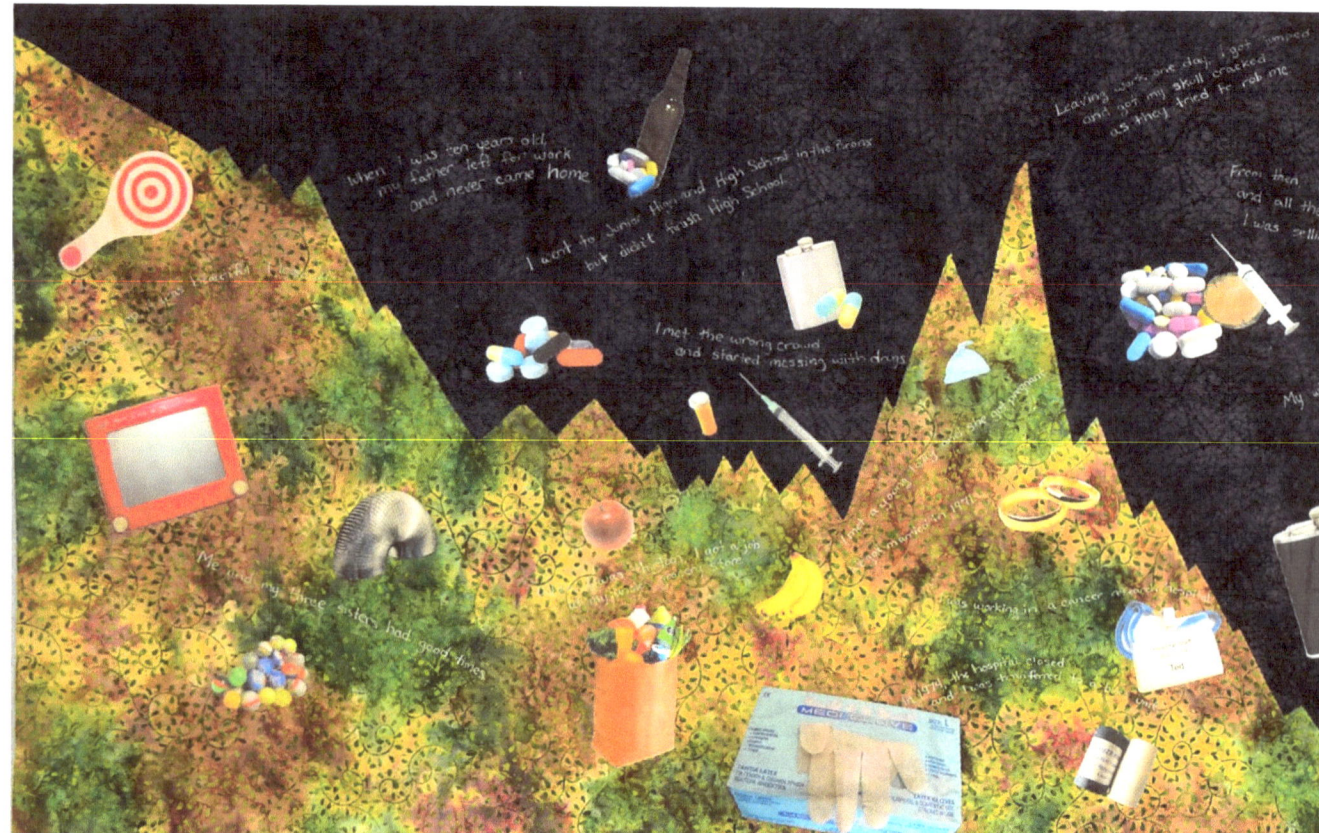

One day, as he was leaving work, a group tried to rob him and cracked his skull in the process. From that point on, he couldn't perform at work and turned to drugs in order to ease the pain. Shortly after that, his wife got pregnant with someone else, so he felt he had to leave. This drove him deeper into drugs. He said, "The devil had me and I didn't know it."

Finally, he escaped the pull of drugs and went to a homeless shelter. He spent 14 months with Ready Willing and Able, and then found work as a cook and a home health aide. Just when he thought he had pulled his life back together and was about to move into his own apartment, he was hit by a car. In physical therapy every day and unable to work, he missed the opportunity to move into the apartment that was offered and had to stay at the shelter a little while longer.

Now ready to return to work and his life, he is thankful for all those in the faith-based shelter who helped him get back on his feet and hopes that another apartment opens soon.

*At his request, Ted's name has been changed.

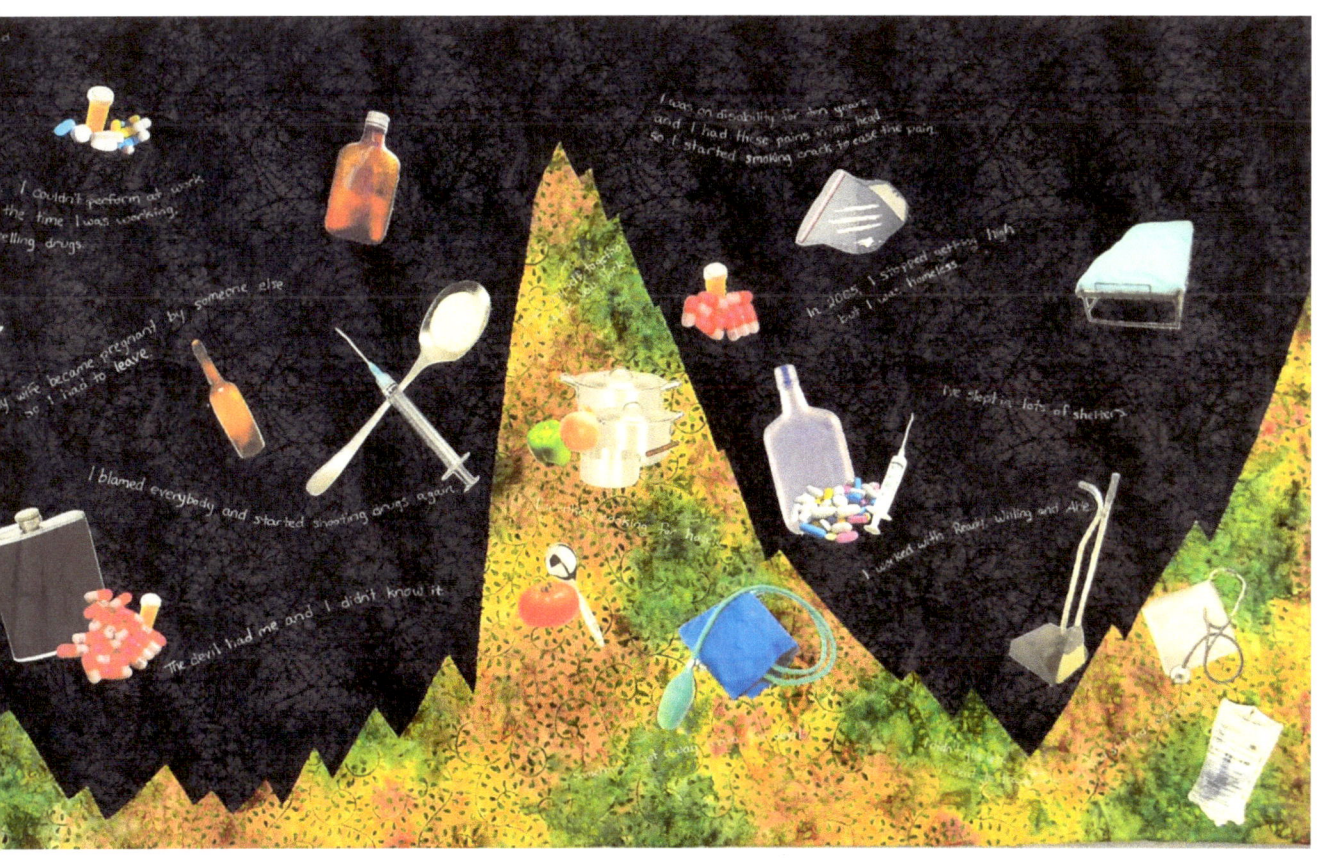

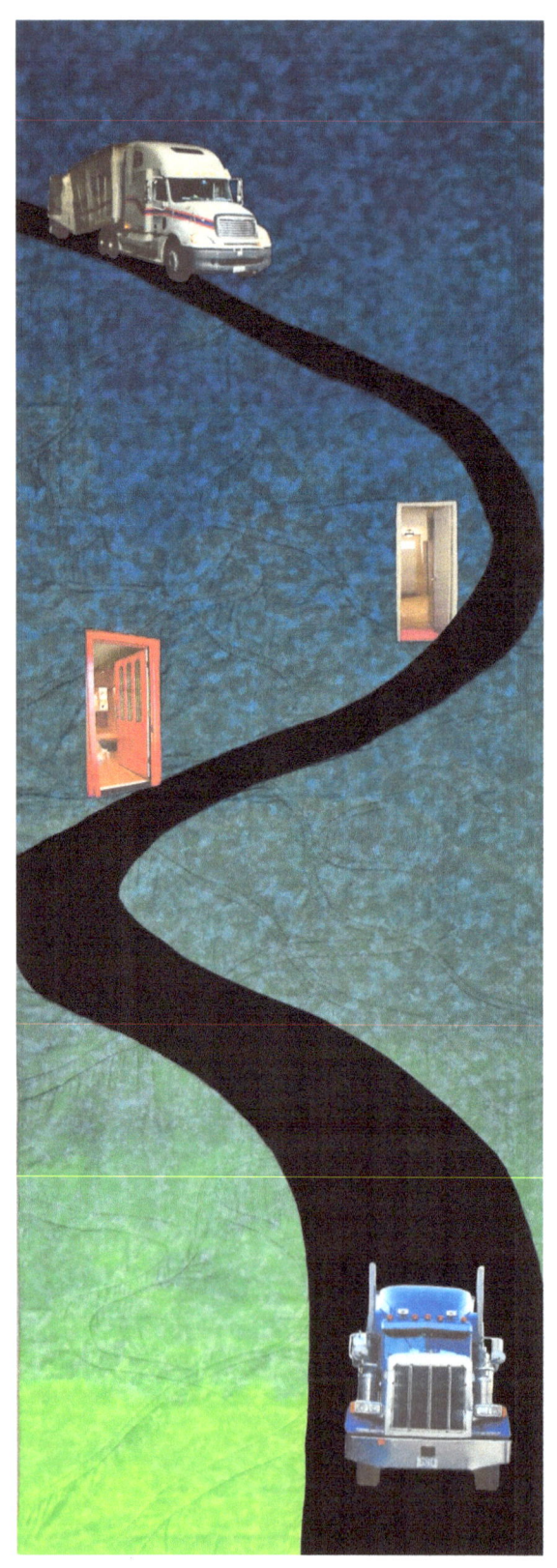

JOHN*

John is a trucker. After getting his truck stuck under a bridge, he lost his job and soon after, could no longer afford rent. John's two daughters (both married and living in the Bronx) invited him to stay with them until he got back on his feet, but John didn't want to be a burden or interfere with their lives. Instead, he decided to enter the shelter system.

People with trucking licenses are in high demand, so John was confident that he would be back on his feet soon. When we spoke, he had a few interviews lined up and hoped that he would not be in the shelter for much longer.

The piece shows his journey on the open road. The damaged truck at the top of the piece is merely another curve in the journey of his life. The two open doors represent the homes of his daughters that he decided to bypass and the truck at the bottom represents his return to the road and his life. In the background of the piece, meandering roads are quilted in clear thread (see below). We all get distracted by the winding paths life takes us on, but with focus and determination like John's, we can pave a path and follow it to our desired destinations.

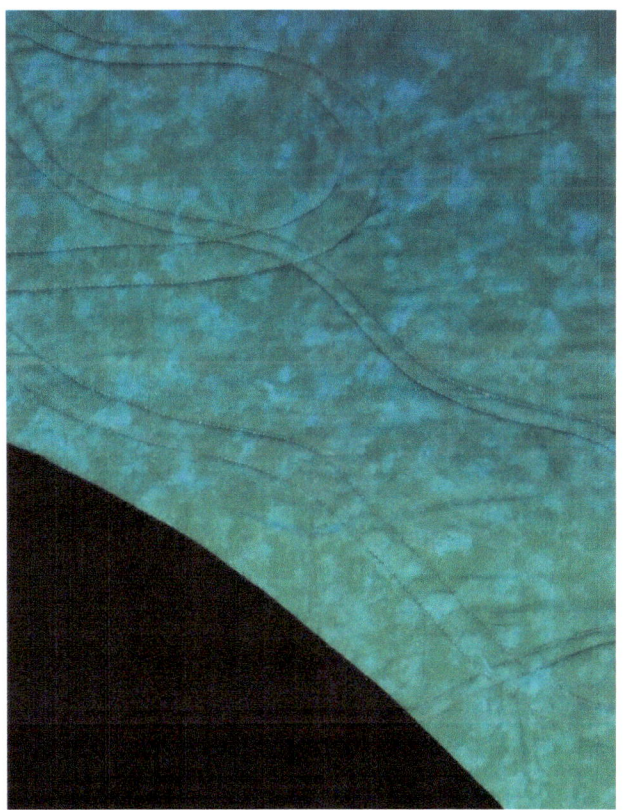

*At his request, John's name has been changed.

Kim

Kim came to New York to escape an abusive relationship. She said she was "tired of fighting for [her] home and [her] safety." She moved to New York and stayed in a drop-in center for 30 days before going to stay with a relative in Las Vegas. Finding out fairly quickly that living with this relative was not a long-term solution, she returned to New York City and the shelter system, finally finding a place in a faith-based shelter.

Her journey to New York (and in the shelter system) is one of healing. She plans to finish her associate degree in business and get her life back on track. In the meantime, she is working as a host for a restaurant and hoping to find a place of her own soon.

To show her journey, the piece features a distressed looking black fabric with rough holes that allow the red fabric behind to show through. As the piece moves from left to right, the holes get smaller and less frequent as she heals. The quilting pattern also reflects this move from chaos to order. The free motion machine quilting transitions from harsh random lines to a grid pattern as the piece moves from the left to the right. A detail of the quilting is shown on the right.

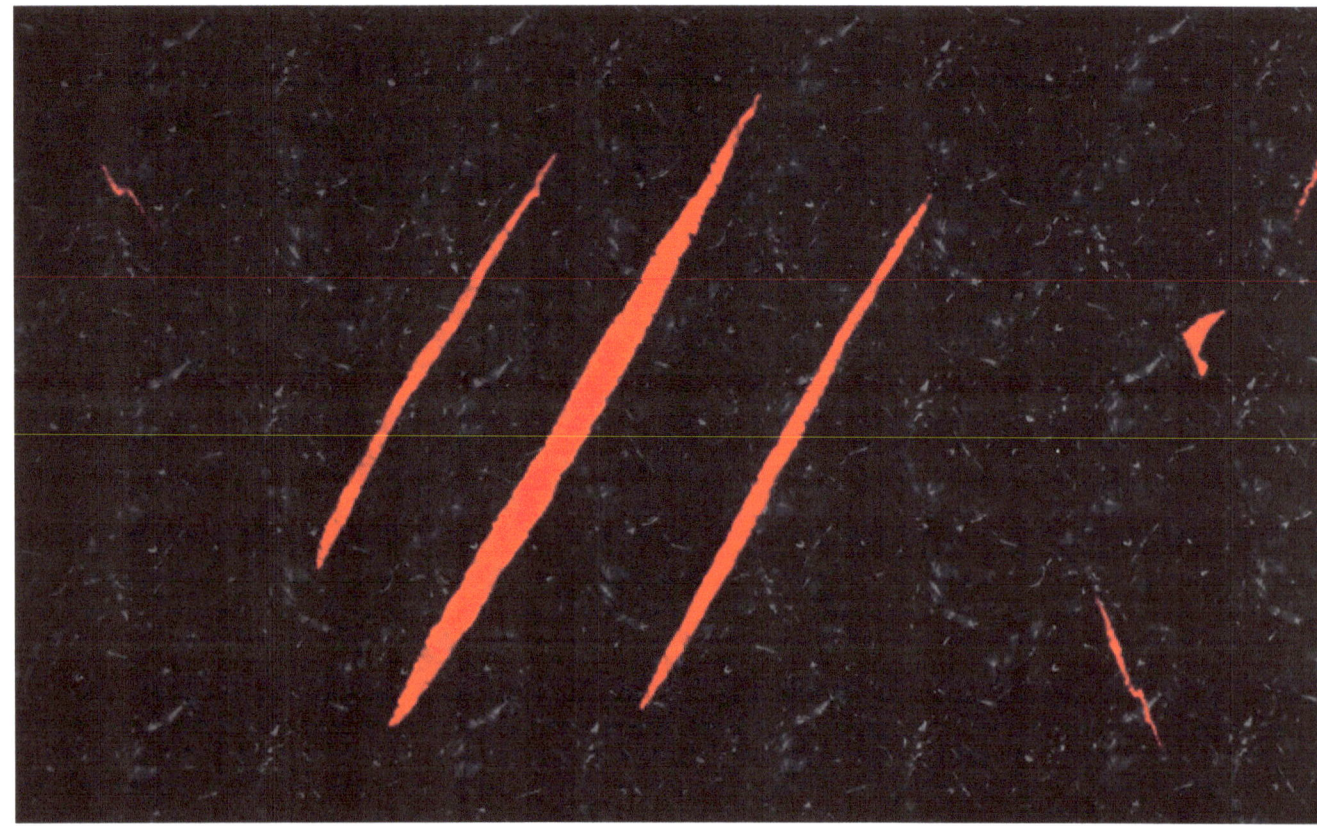

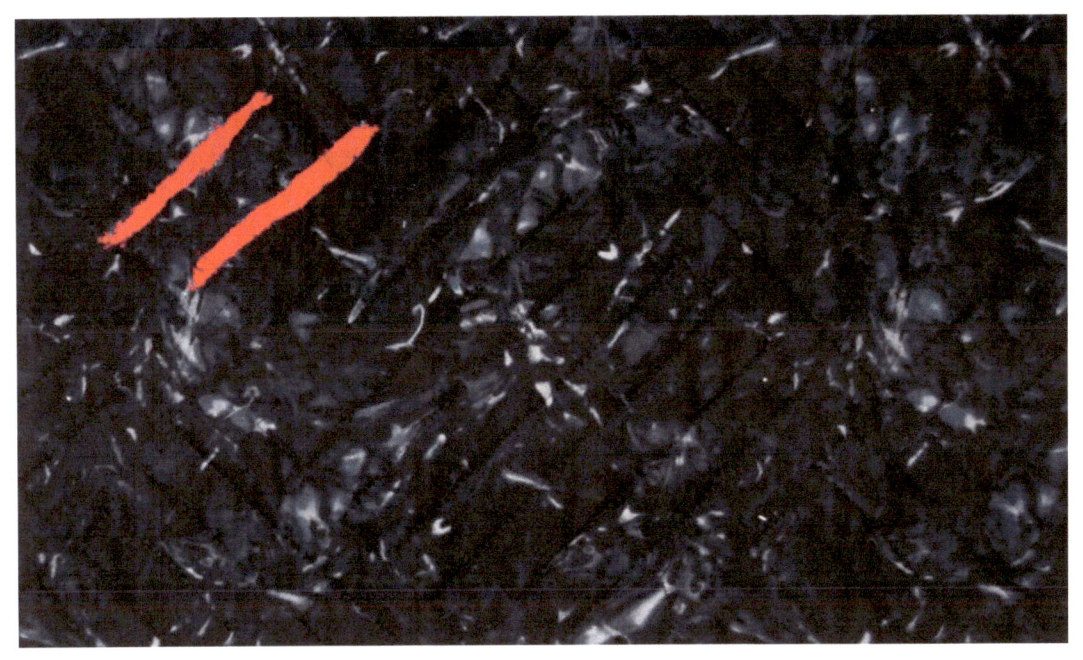

ERIC*

Eric was a manager in a hotel when the economy crashed and he was laid off in 2007. Suddenly, after 25 years working in the business, he was unemployed. For almost a year, he walked the streets with resume in hand looking for a job. He literally wore out several pairs of shoes, but found nothing.

Finally, in 2008, he was no longer able to pay rent and other bills so one night, he left his apartment, closed the door behind him and got on a bus. He got off that bus and boarded another, unsure where to go. As the night grew colder, he decided to call 311 where he learned about three drop-in centers. He recognized the name of one as a place where he used to volunteer with his son.

He walked to the first center on the list and watched from afar as people went in and out. He couldn't bring himself to go in, so he went to the next and walked by it several times before gathering the strength to enter. Not ready to accept a shelter bed, he stayed in the drop-in center for months, sleeping on one of their waiting room chairs. During this time, he was diagnosed with thyroid cancer and had surgery. When he returned to the center, he decided to try a church bed and was "extremely overjoyed" to meet the shelter coordinators where he saw how they extended themselves to welcome the shelter guests. He found that the other men in the shelter were like a "band of brothers" and they all looked out for each other.

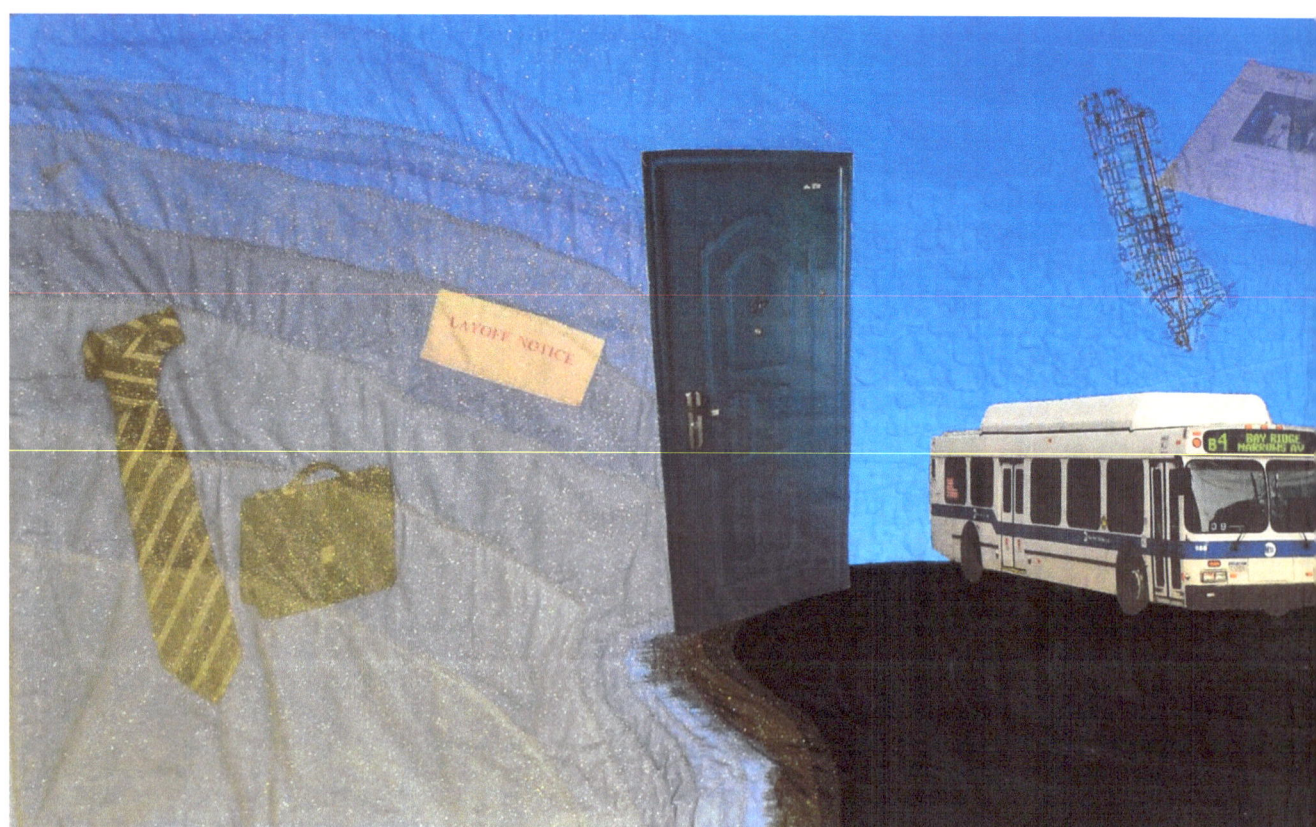

Shortly after accepting the shelter bed, he returned to college for a business degree and found solace there. When he wasn't at the shelter or in class, he would spend his time in the public library and always carried around the New York Times. While he waits for his call to get housing, he lends a listening ear to the others in the shelter and tries to focus on his future.

The left side of the piece represents Eric's old life with an apartment, tie, and briefcase behind layers of sheer fabric. The center of the piece features the city bus that took him away from that life hovering above a black vortex with his new life of the bus map, shelter cot, public library, and cancer cells above. To the right is the helping hand he found through the faith-based shelter and the mountain that he still has to climb – but not alone.

*At his request, Eric's name has been changed.

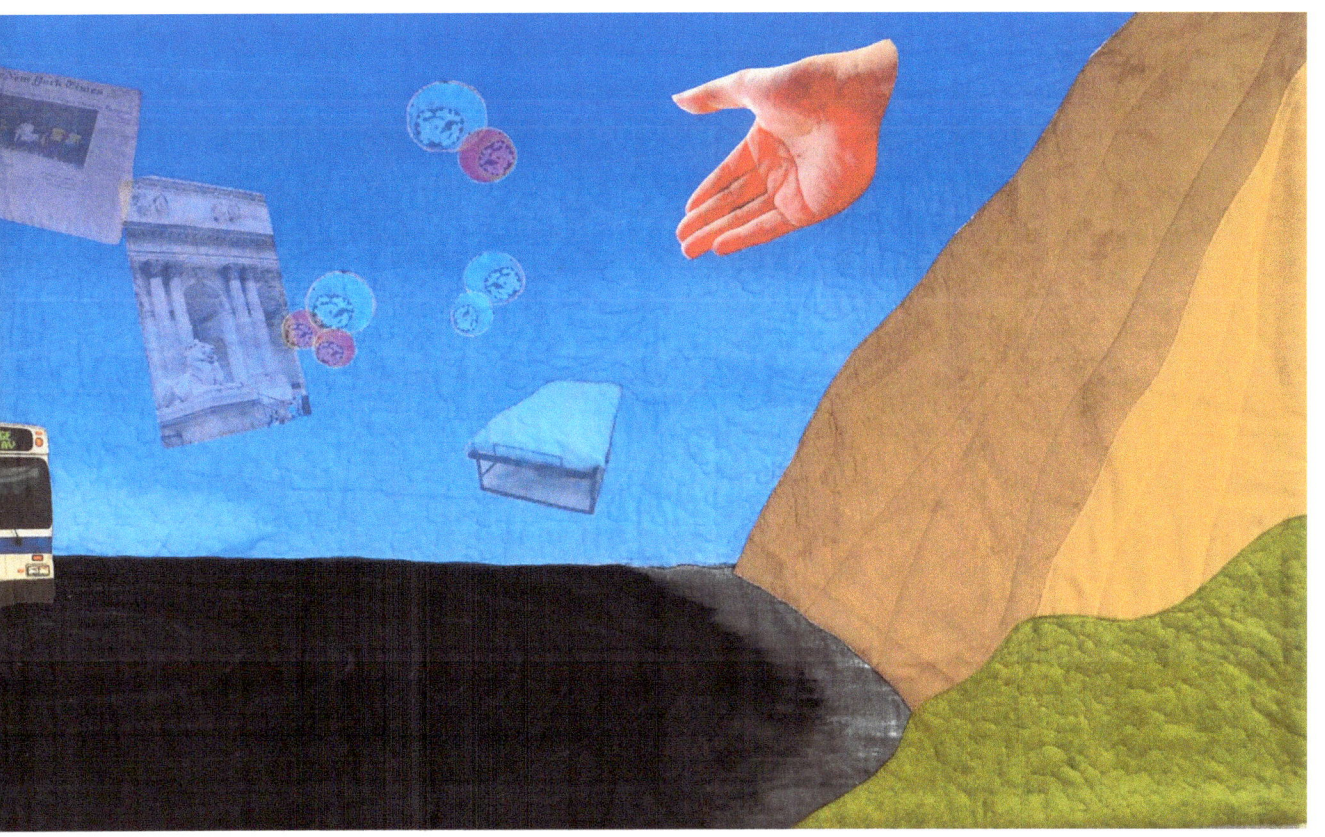

OUTSIDE WALLS:
ART BY CHILDREN IN NEW YORK'S FAMILY SHELTERS

UNIVERSITY FAMILY RESIDENCE
BRONX, NY

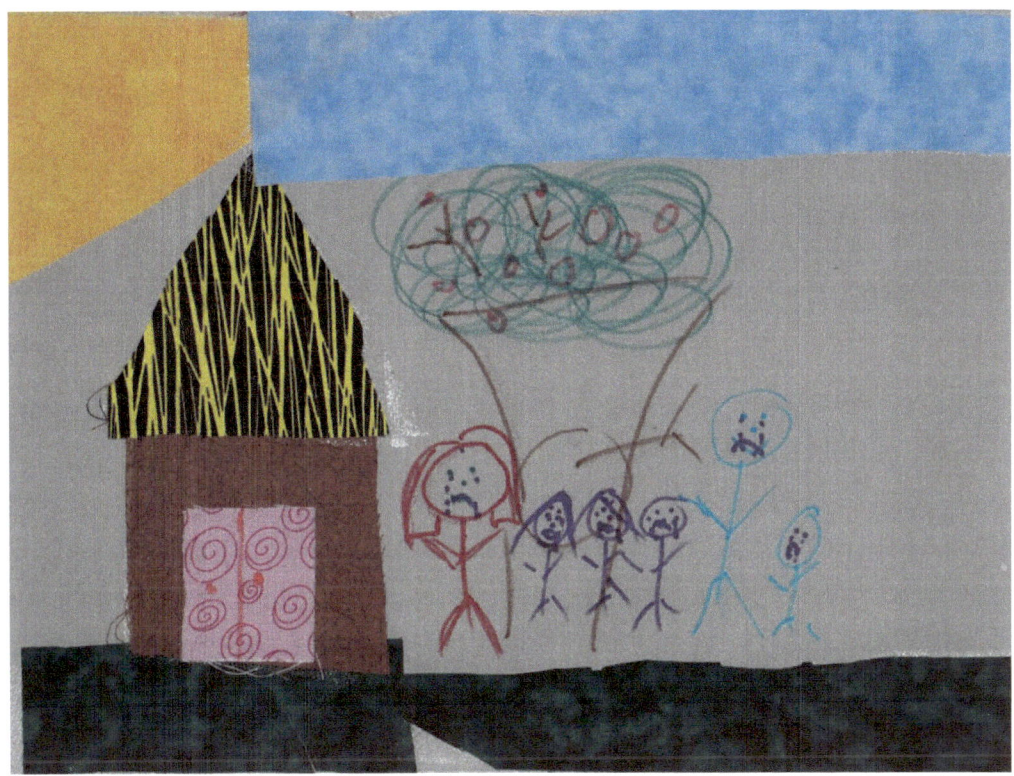

Jereco, age 9

Jereco has been living at the University Family Residence with his three siblings for about a year. He created his piece about the day he left their house. "I cried the day we had to leave," he said.

His piece shows him with his family standing outside their old house crying because they had to move away.

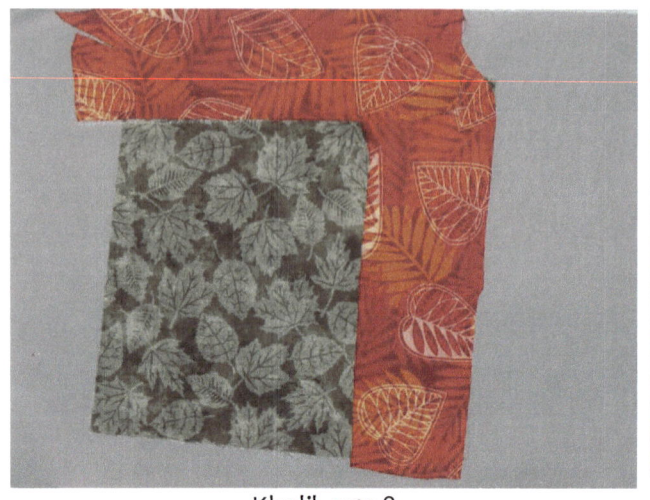

Khalil, age 8

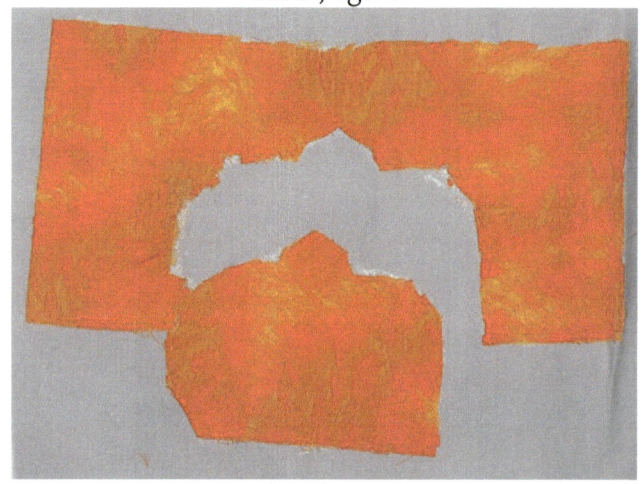

Nakiya, age 10

Miguel, age 9

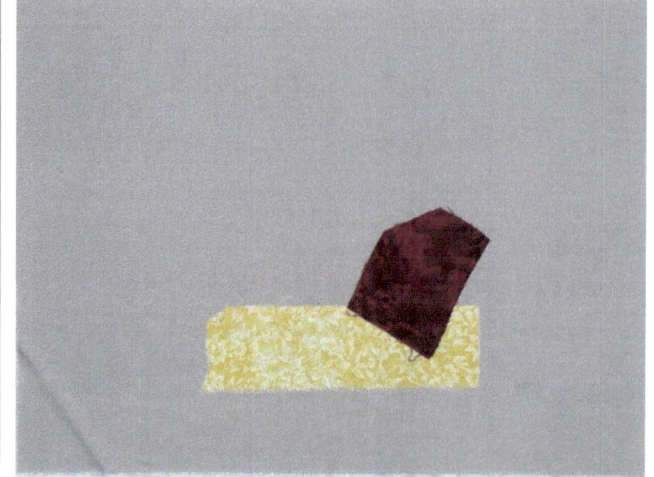

Majid, age 7.5

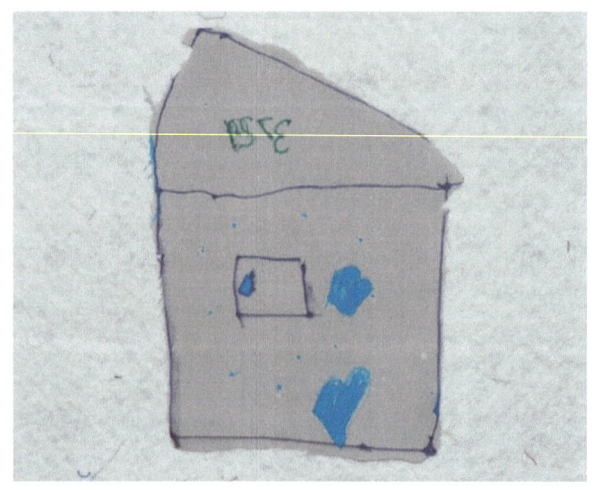

Simone, age 6

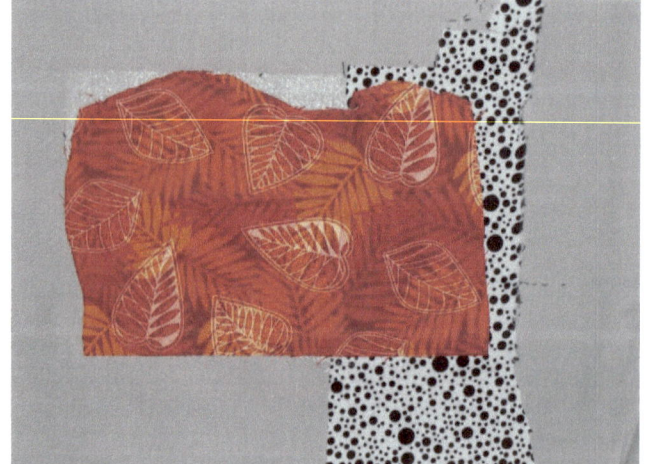

Kanika, age 6

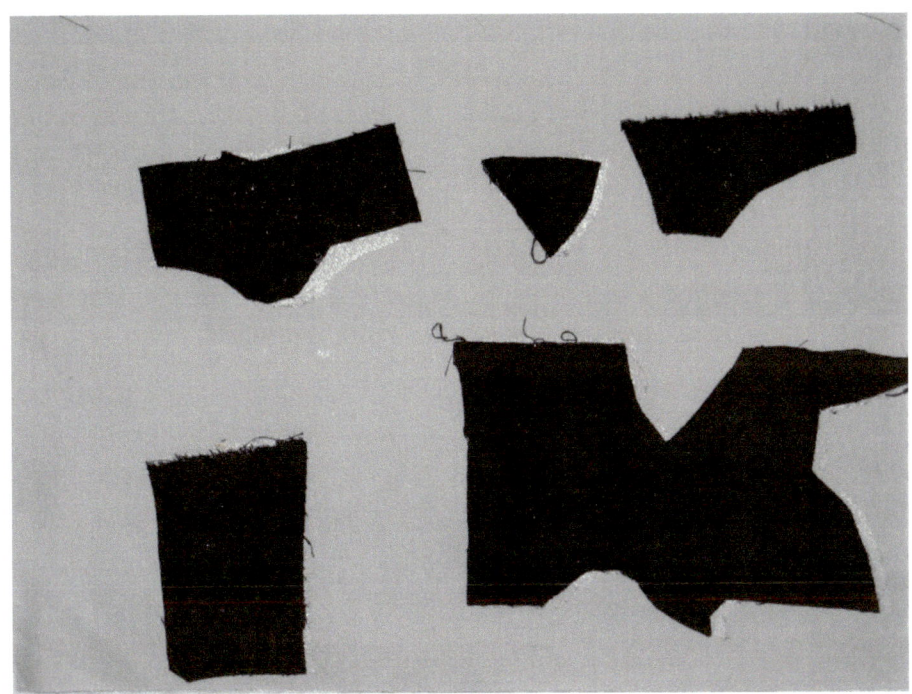

Jonathan, age 7, told me that living in the shelter makes him angry. "I'm mad that I have to be here." He chose to use black shapes with sharp angles to represent his anger.

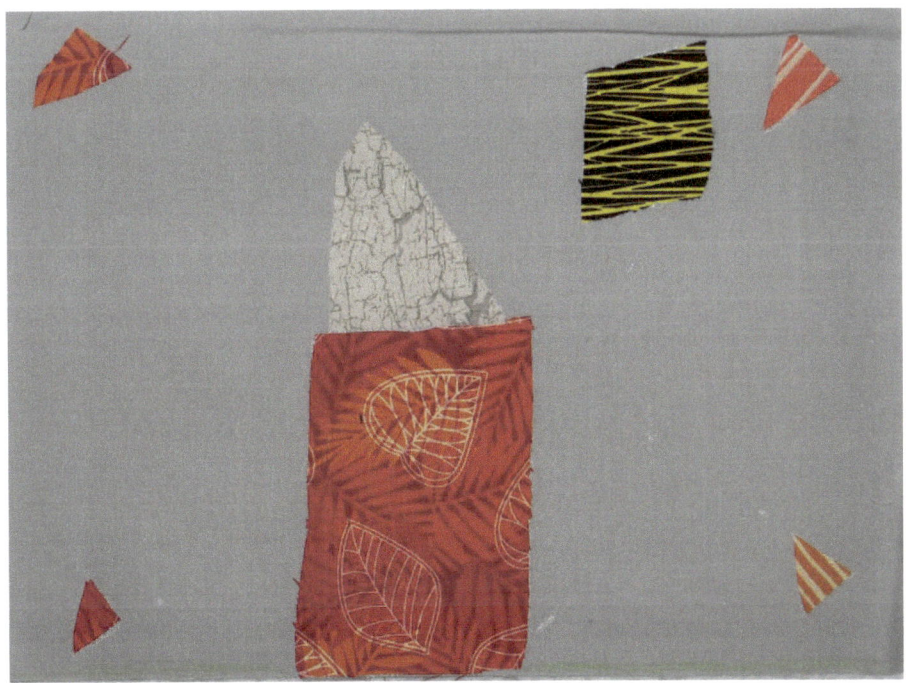

Brenton, age 8, was happy to move to the University Family Residence because it was quiet when compared to the Manhattan shelter where he lived previously with his mother and sister. His picture is of "the house where [he's] going to live someday way out in the country where it's quiet." He used red and orange in the piece to show his excitement about the move to a different shelter.

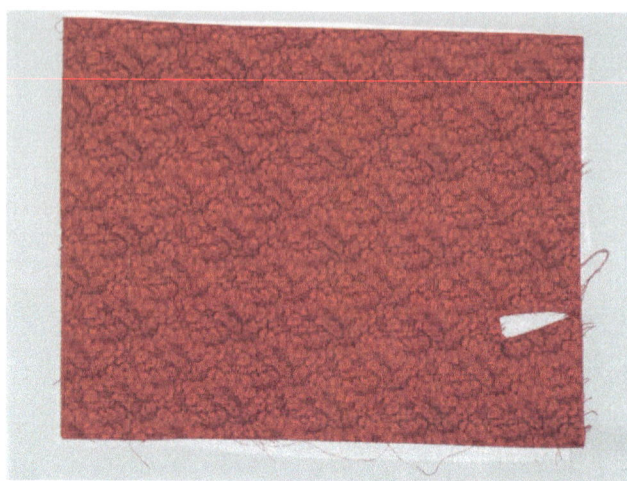

Rashid, age 11, has been living in the shelter for two and a half years with his mother and brother. He feels sad and alone living in the shelter and feels "different from everyone in [his] class."

He said, "My mother left with us because we had some problems with our family. When we left with my mother I felt sad, alone, and had a sick feeling in my stomach."

Although he identified black, blue, white and grey as the colors of sadness and loneliness, he decided to create his piece completely in red.

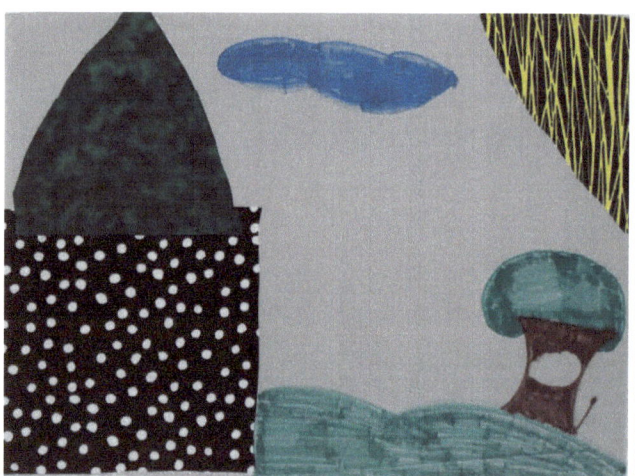

Irma, age 11

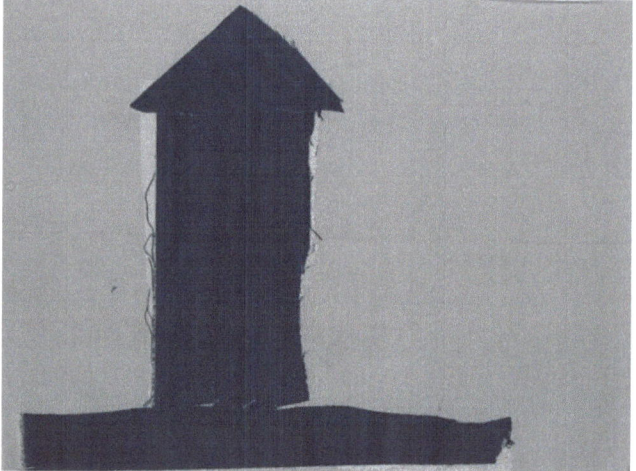

Keimary, age 6

Kanika, age 6, lives in the shelter with her mother and brother. She has moved several times in her six years; so many that she has lost count.

While she doesn't like living in the shelter, she does like her school. In this piece, Kanika drew a picture of herself walking in the rain.

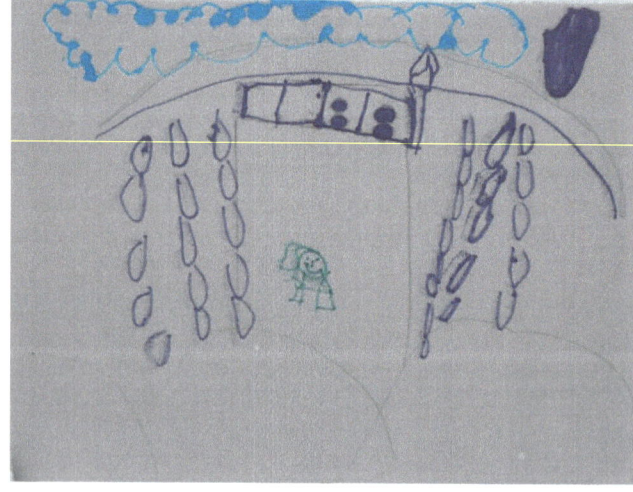

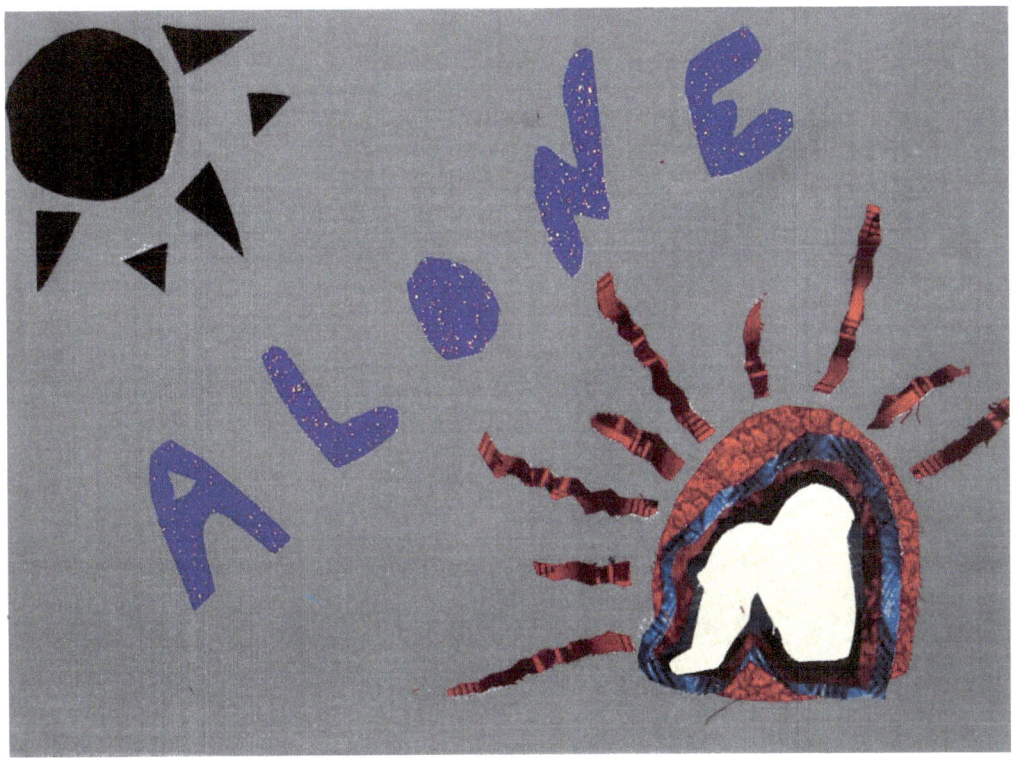

Haille, age 14

Haille lives in the shelter with her mother. Before moving there, they were living with her grandmother. She said, "When I came here, my mother wouldn't let me talk to anyone. No one to talk to, no one to understand. Just all alone. By myself."

She created a piece that shows her "true self" as the glittery figure covered with darkness under a black sun.

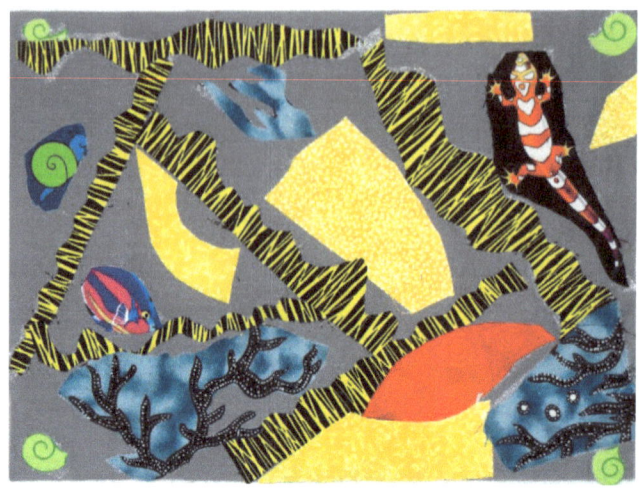

Kalia, age 19, moved into the shelter 19 days before our workshop. She is on her own and 6 months pregnant.

She is thankful to have a roof over her head until she can find a place of her own and feels like she's "making the transition from child to adult" as she moves from college life to responsible adult and mother.

Her piece represents a light at the end of a tunnel.

Todiah, age 14, was also new to Springfield Family Residence and had mixed feelings about living there.

In her piece, the green represents her life before the shelter which was "ok but not great." There were some good times in that old life, shown by the yellow block. "Then it got bad" represented by the black square, followed by a series of ups and downs shown by the colored dots.

She believes that things will be good again, so the yellow block in the top right shows that bright future.

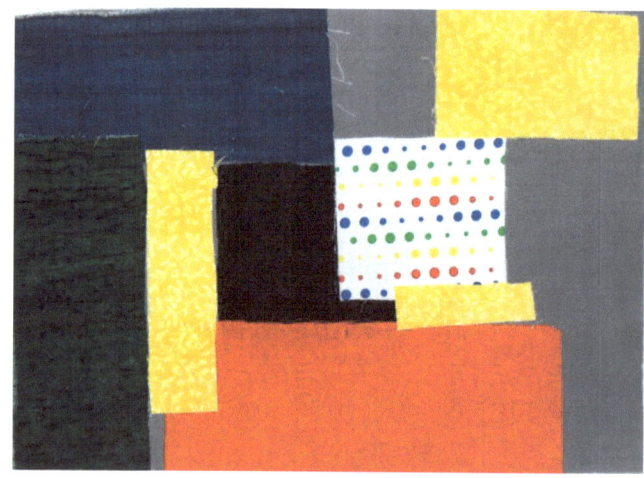

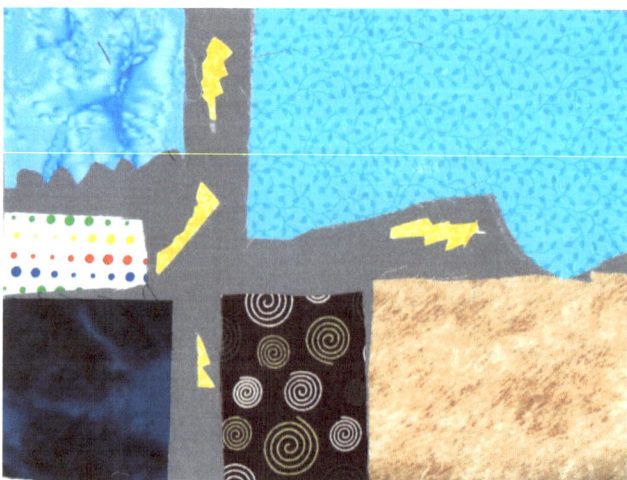

Leeann, age 13, lives in the shelter with her mother and sister. She said the shelter feels "like jail" and she is angry about living there. There are, however, some good sides because she gets to meet new people.

In her piece, the blue blocks and lightning bolts represent "the evil" and the brown represents her mixed feelings about living in the shelter.

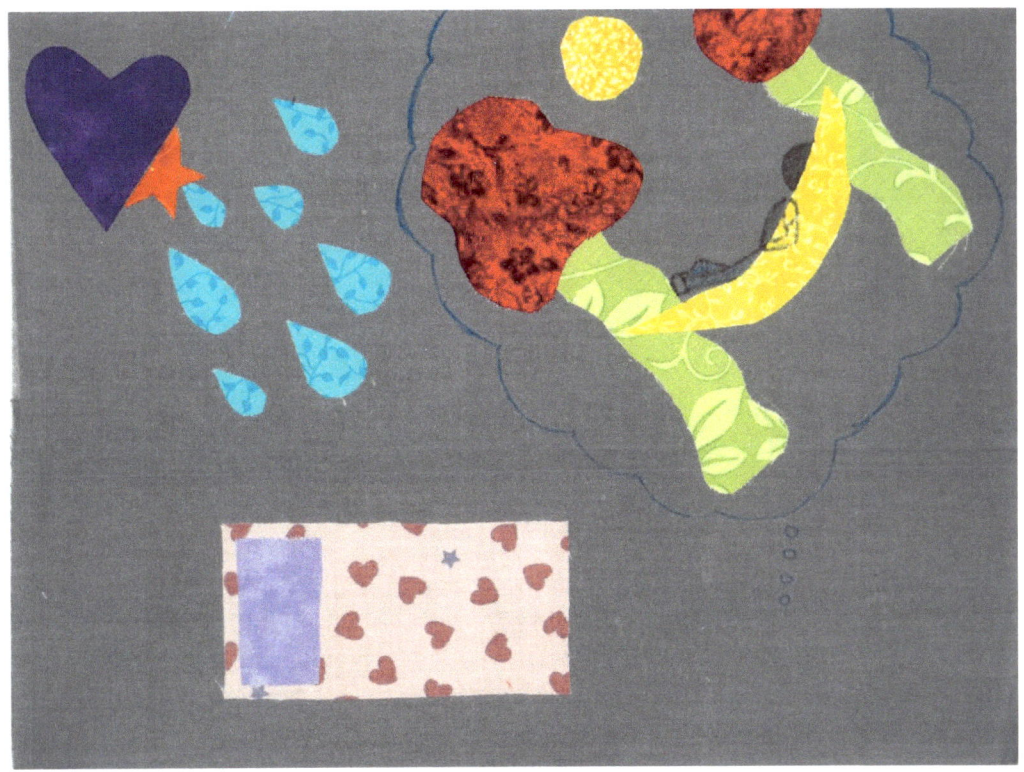
Melanie, age 19

Melanie has been living in the shelter for 4 months with her 9-month-old son. She is 6 months pregnant and trying to find a way to make it on her own. Her mother and brother live in the City, but she has several more siblings and a father in Puerto Rico where she was born.

She said that living in the shelter is "difficult because you don't have any of your family members. I feel like I'm doing the right thing for me and my son... My experiences being homeless have taught me how to be thankful for what I already have."

Her piece shows a picture of her bed at the shelter with a dream bubble of life relaxing in Puerto Rico.

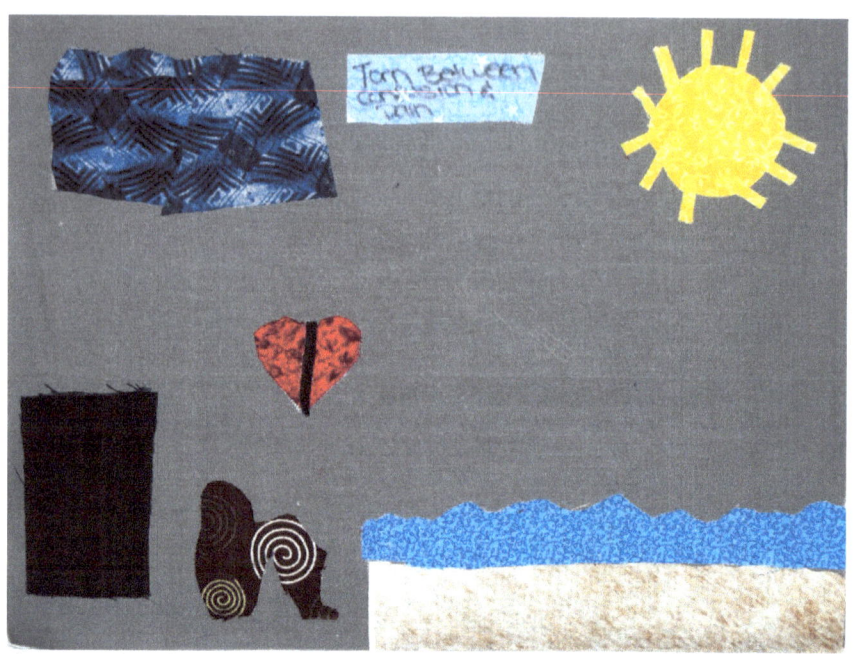

Elizabeth, age 17 lives in the shelter with her mother and sister. Living there has been frustrating for her. She said, "I feel like I'm under lockdown and can't go out and do anything. I feel like I'm 5 again and not 17. Being in a shelter is one of the hardest things anyone could go through."

"On the other hand," she continued, "it can teach you to be independent and learn the values of the little things you have." Her piece shows her mixed feelings about living in the shelter: happiness for a place to live alongside pain and frustration.

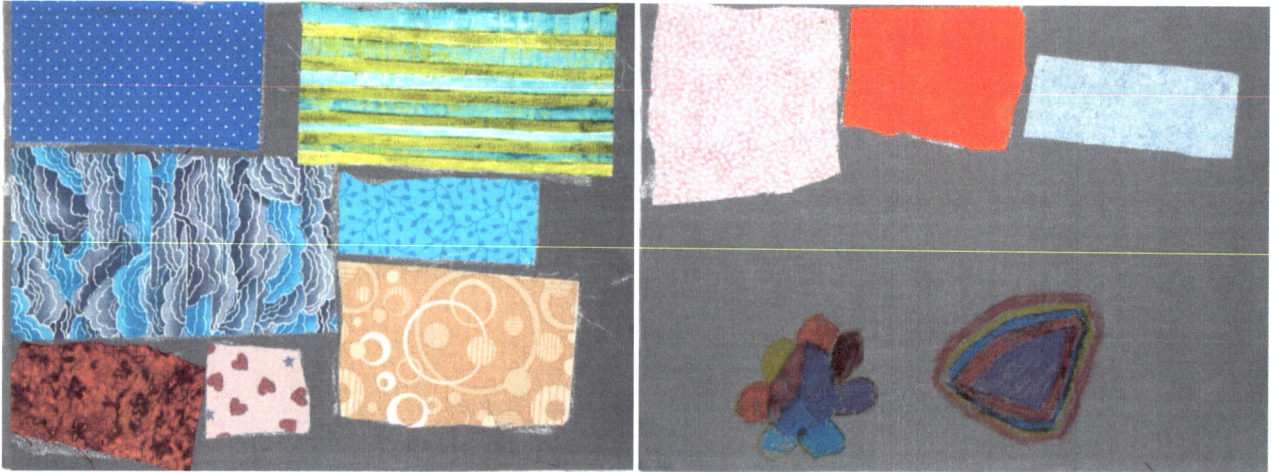

Tiffanty, age 9, has been living in the shelter for one month with her mother and grandmother. Living there makes her sad, so she made two pieces using the colors she sees as representing sadness.

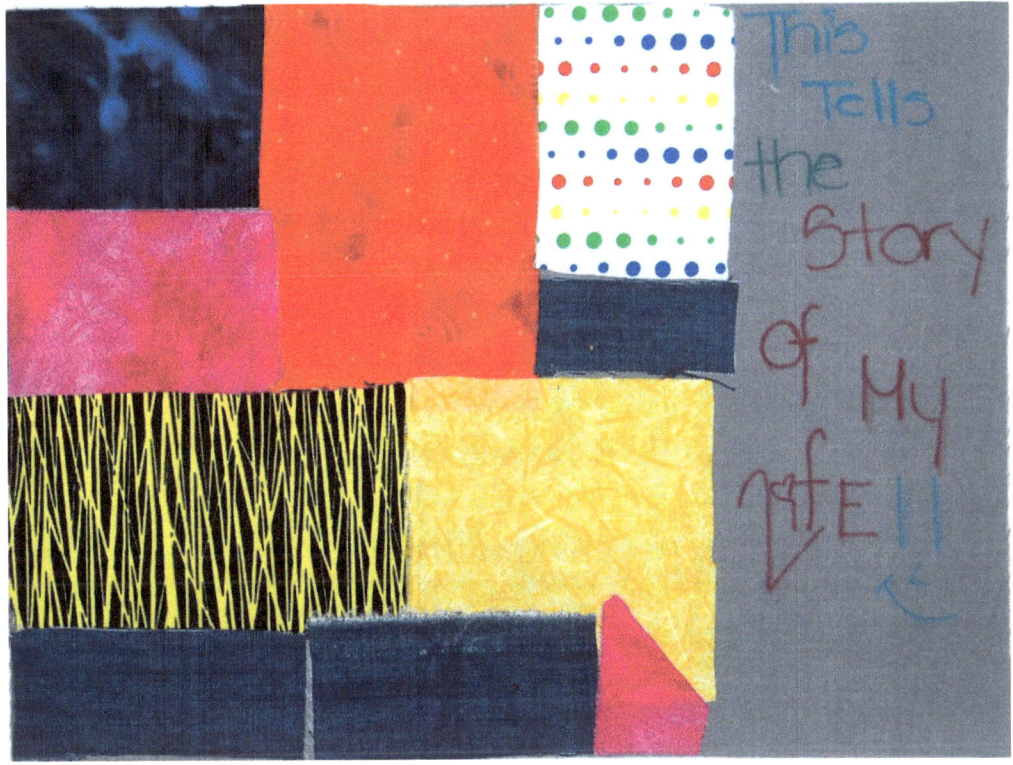

Anasia, age 13

Anasia lives in the shelter with her mother, father, two sisters and nephew. She said, "It's kind of hard to live in a shelter, but it's better than living on the street."

She created a piece that expresses her mixed feelings about life in the shelter: embarrassment, fear, happiness, anger, loneliness, sadness, exhaustion, shame and sorrow. Each color in the piece represents a different emotion.

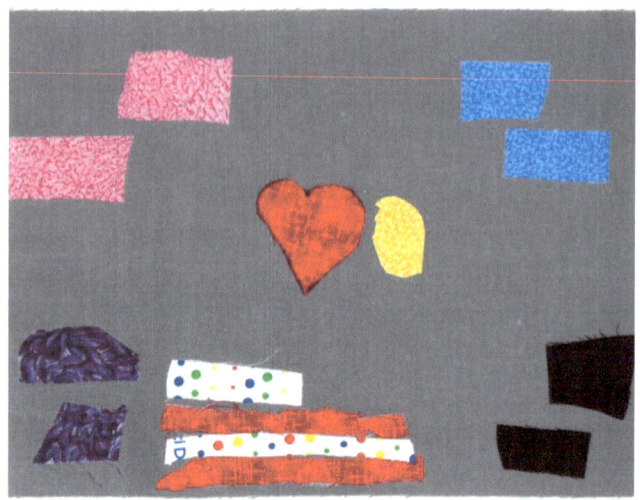
Destiny, age 10

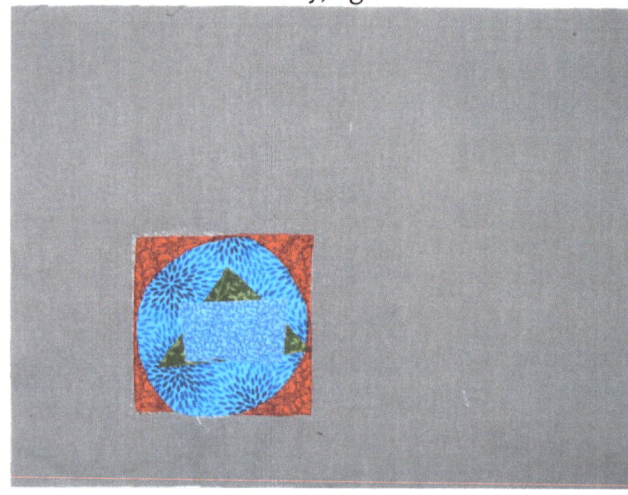
Antonio, age 8

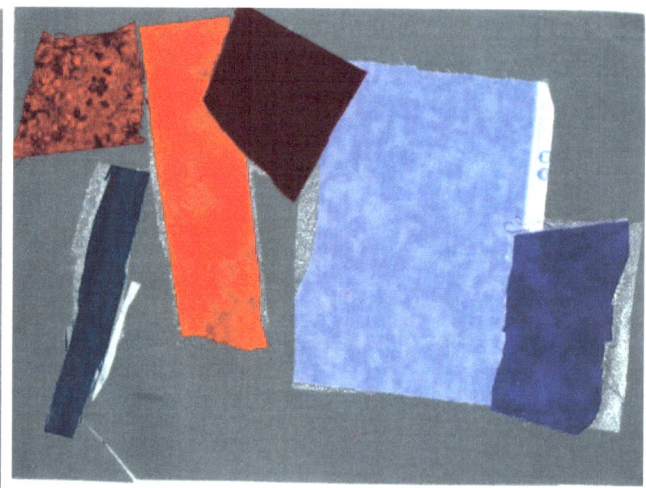
Carlos, age 9

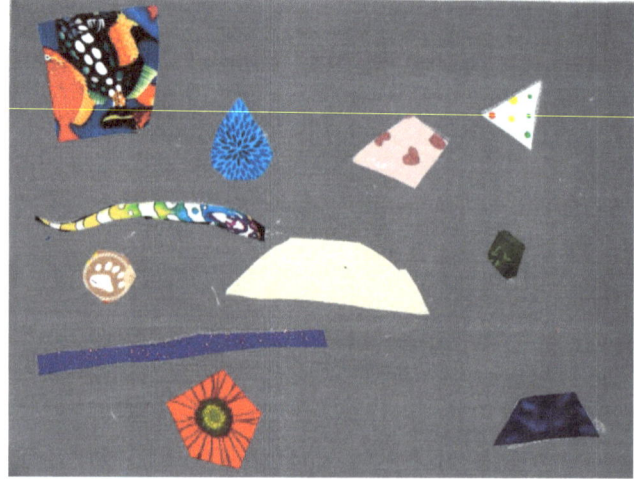
DeAngela, age 10

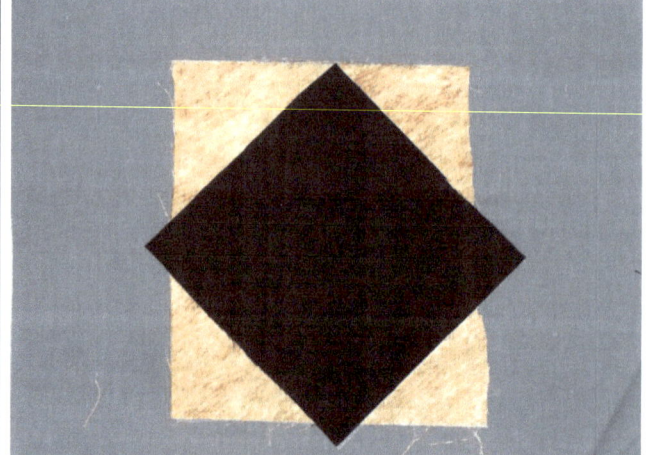
Daevon, age 11

DaShawn, age 11

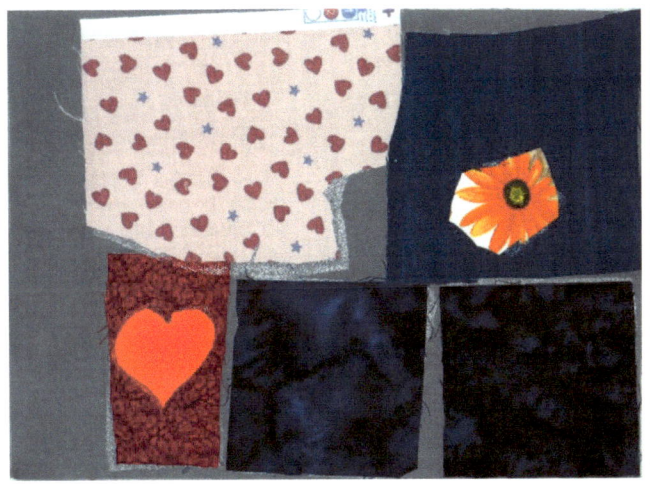

Lesly, age 10

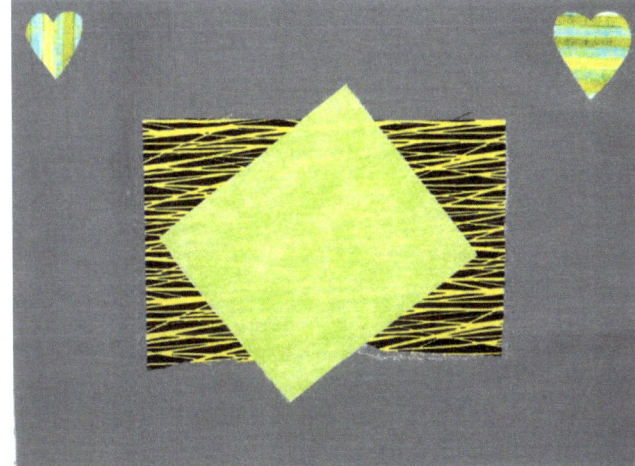

De-Aundre, age 12

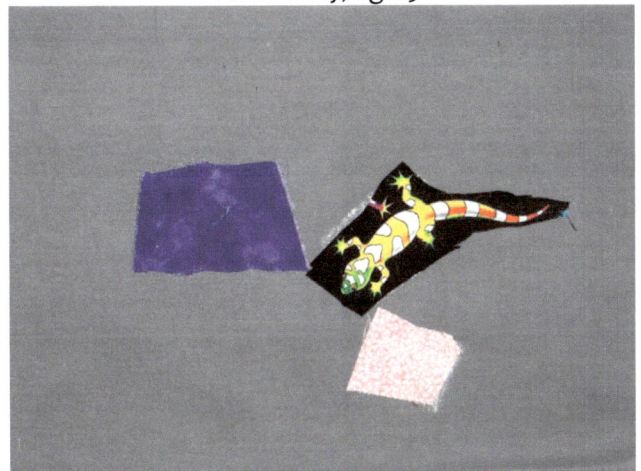

Knachanty, age 9

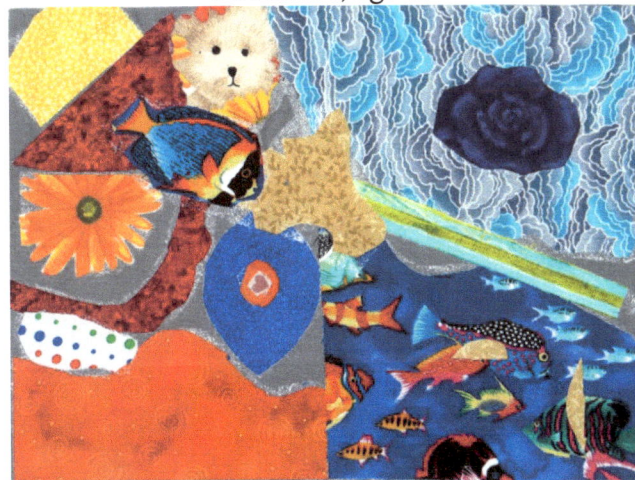

Miss Silvia, Recreation Specialist

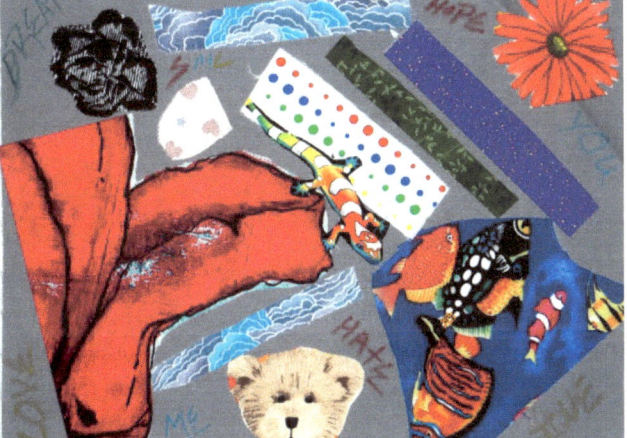

Jefferson, age 8

Miss Doris

37

ABYSSINIAN HOUSE
NEW YORK, NY

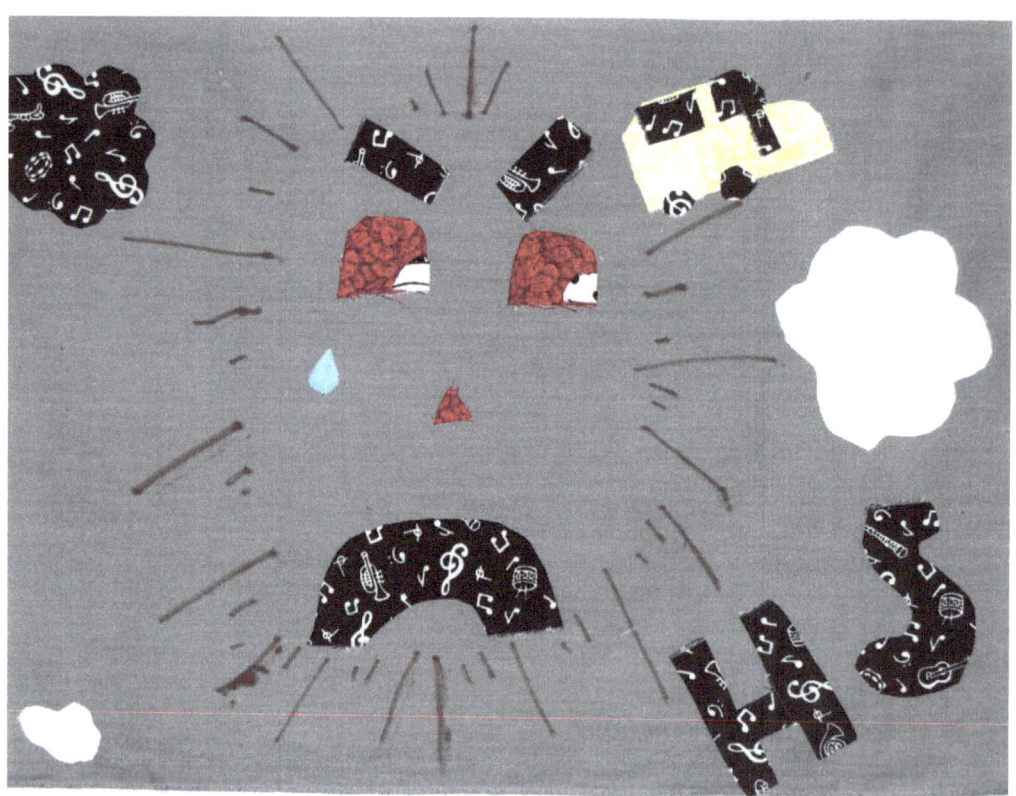

Johanna, age 15

Abyssinian House is the fourth shelter that Johanna, her mother, brother and sister have moved to in the seven months since they left their home in upstate New York. She was angry the day her mother told them they were moving and said that living in the shelter "doesn't feel like home."

She created her piece about her first day at the new secondary school for law. On her first day of school, she passed her stop and ended up all the way out in Coney Island when she had only been three stops from school. Her piece represents the frustration she felt that day complete with a school bus and a blue teardrop.

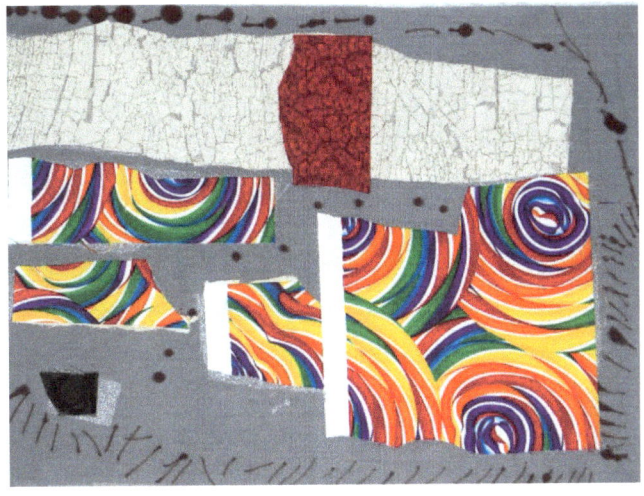

Jada, age 5, lives with her mother, father and three brothers. The day she moved to the shelter, she "felt bad" because she thought her mother was going to prison and she thought shelters were bad. When she arrived, however, she found out that it was a good place.

She chose happy colors to express her relief and how much she enjoys the afterschool program at the shelter.

Meia, age 6, lives with her mother, father, baby sister and big brother. She likes this shelter because they can make their own food and play, but is also sad to switch schools so often. "Being homeless," she said, "you have to switch schools a lot. I switched schools five times. It's sad because I have to make new friends and meet new teachers."

Her piece shows the two sides of her feelings: happiness in the sun with a tree and flowers and fear with monsters and darkness.

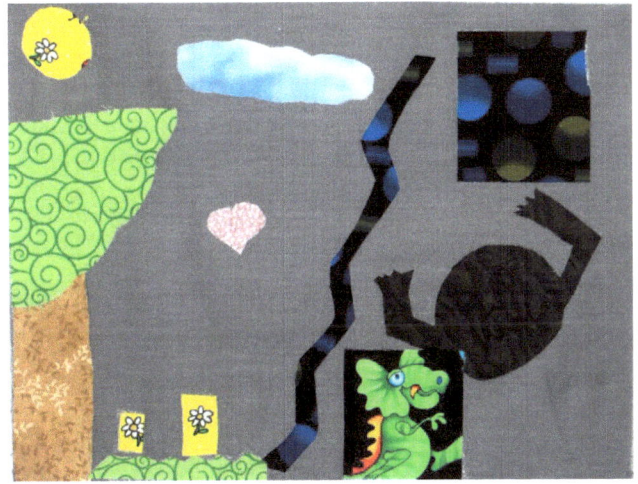

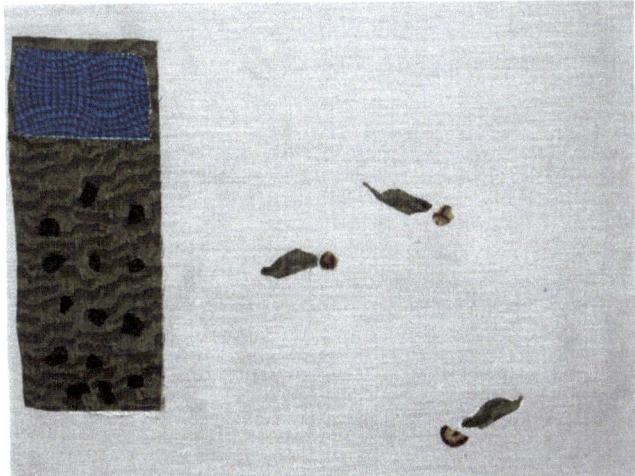

Daniel, age 12, lives with his mother and two sisters. He said, "I don't like living in the shelter because it doesn't feel like home."

He spoke about how the shelter can be a happy place, but chose to show the downside of the shelter with bedbugs and mice.

Alisha, age 7, lives with her mother and father. She likes living in the shelter, but was sad to change schools.

Her piece is about her happiness and the fun they have in the recreation program.

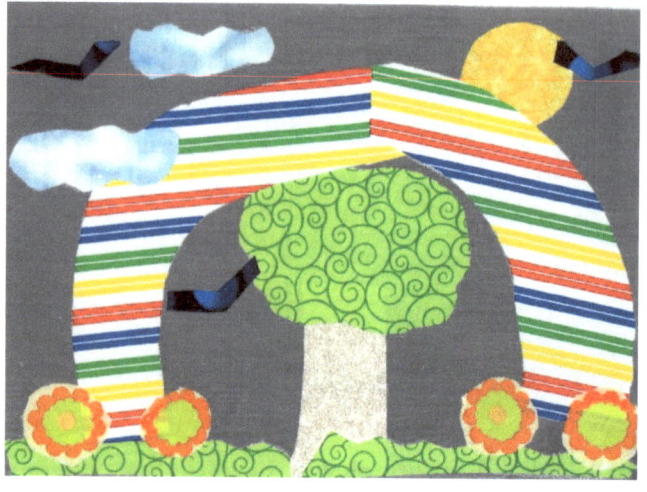

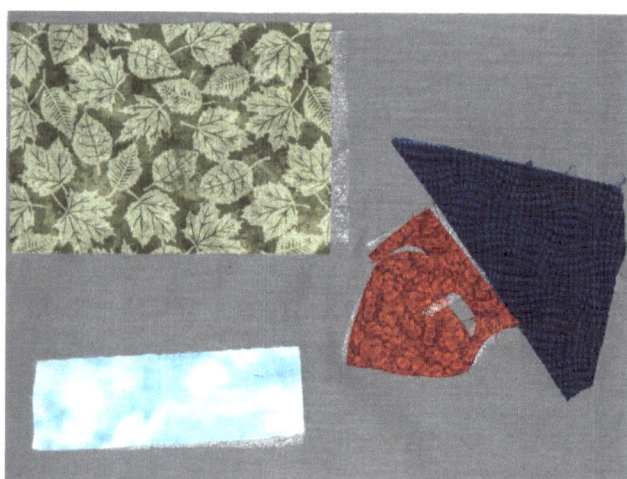

Robert, age 8, lives in the shelter with his father and two baby sisters. He has mixed feelings about the shelter and said that sometimes he is so happy he feels "like doing cartwheels" but at other times he is sad and "every time [he] takes a step [he] feels afraid."

The piece is a self portrait with the blue shape as his bed, the green as the view out the window and his red head wearing a blue hat.

Carl, age 10, lives in the shelter with his mother, father, and sister. He spoke about the day he moved into the shelter and admitted that he "was a little frightened."

His piece shows the before and after of his life. Before, life was like a sunny day with a green tree and grass. Now, all he can see is the lightning bolt that changed everything and barrenness.

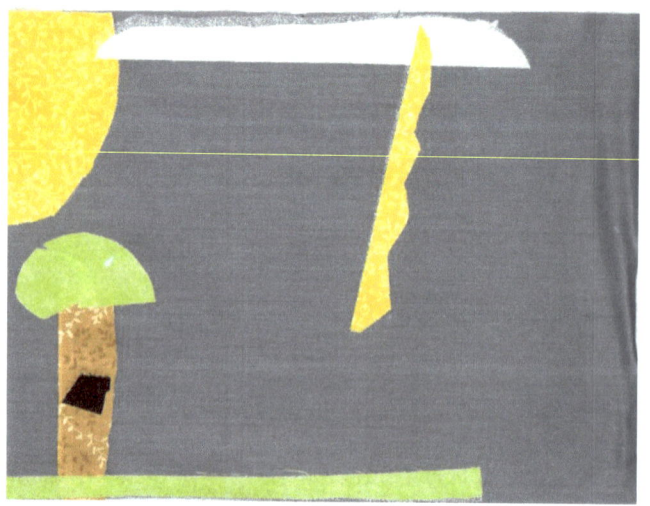

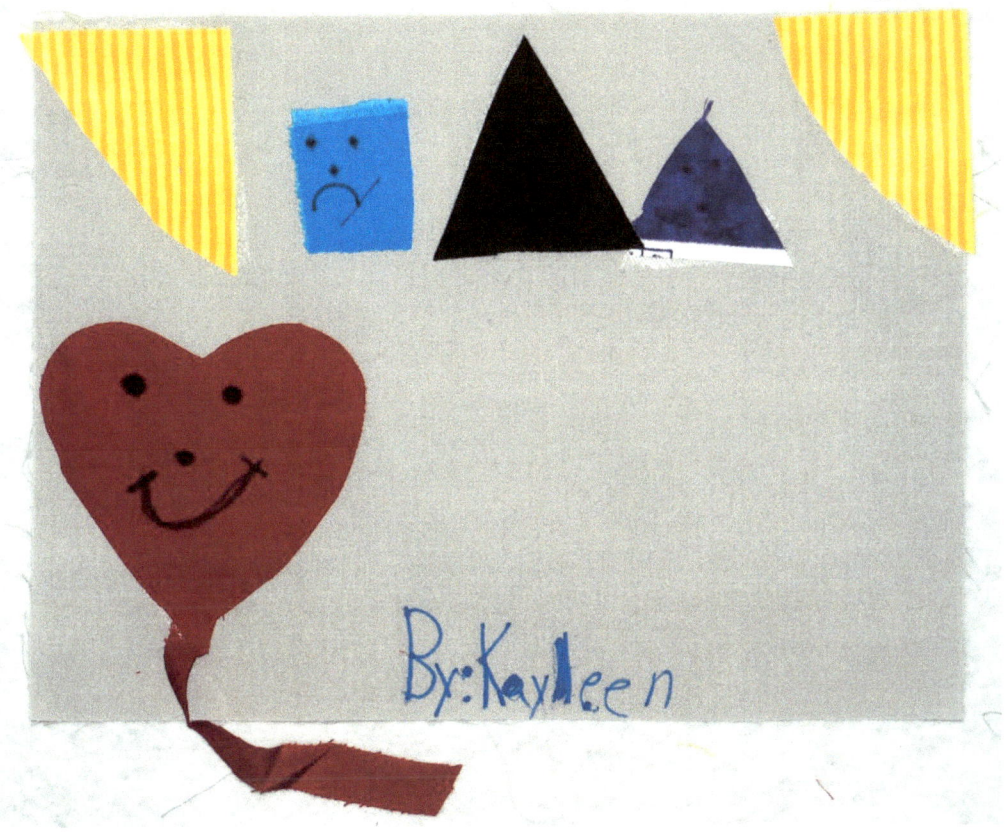

Kayleen, age 9

Kayleen has been living at the Willow Residence with her father for four months. She talked about her fears and worries. She said, "My dad couldn't always get money for food and I was scared and sad." Now, she feels comfortable in the shelter and doesn't worry as much.

Each color in her piece has a different meaning. The blue square is about her sadness because she was hungry, the back triangle shows her fear about not knowing where food would come from and the purple triangle represents her nervousness. The red heart balloon symbolizes her happiness and her feeling that she is now able to take off and thrive in a worry-free life.

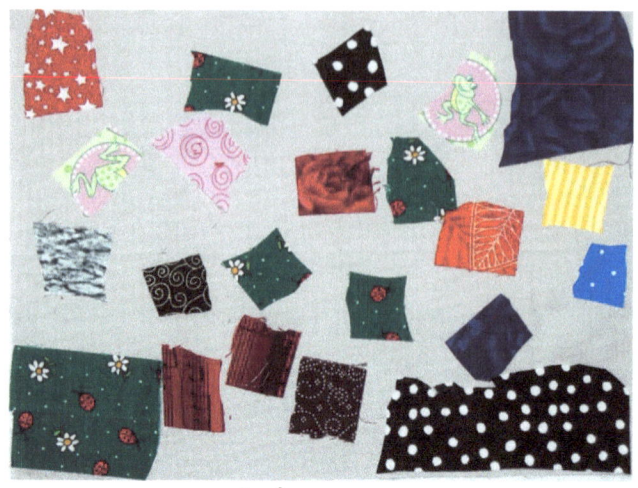

Andrea, age 5

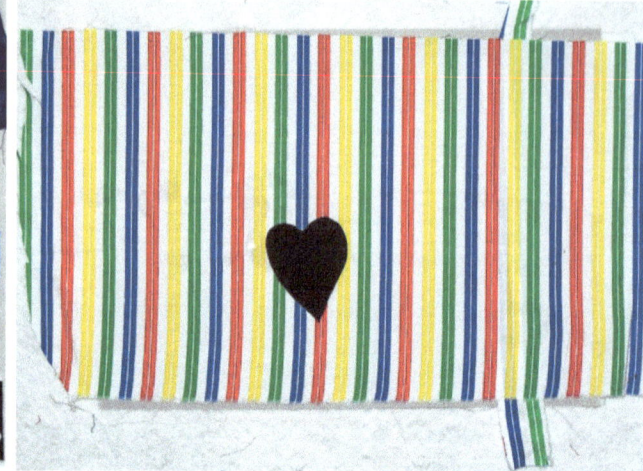

John, age 6

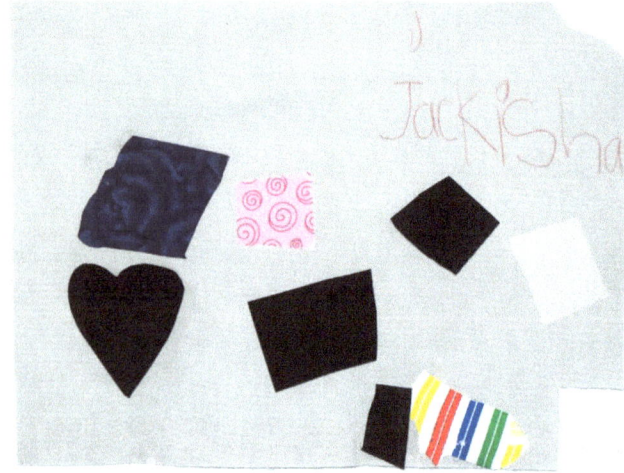
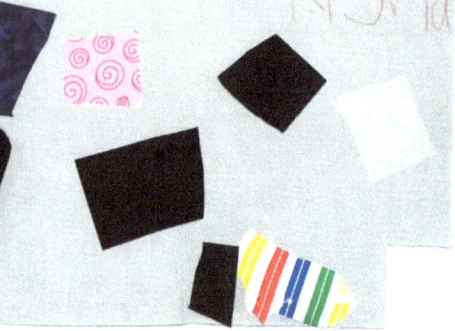

Jackisha, age 5

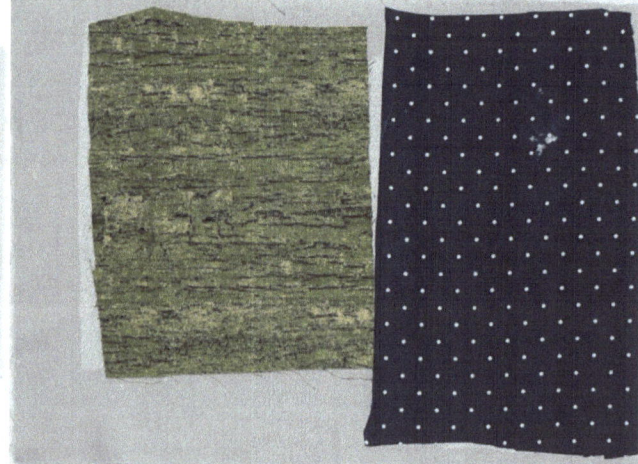

Cristian, age 11

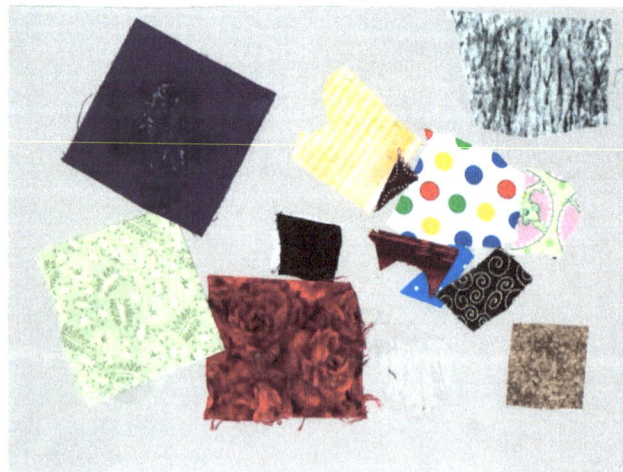

Jason, age 6

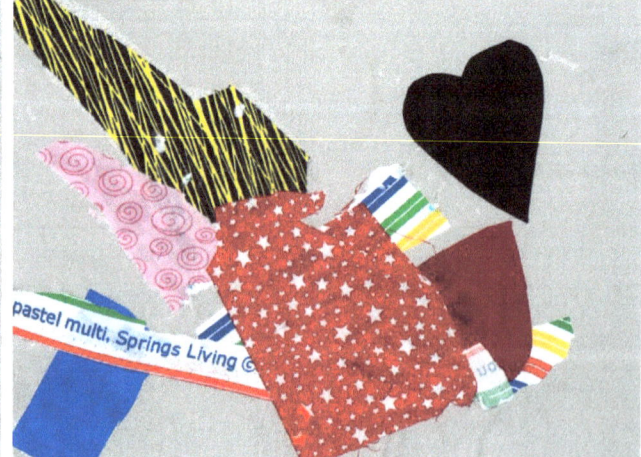

Wayne, age 8

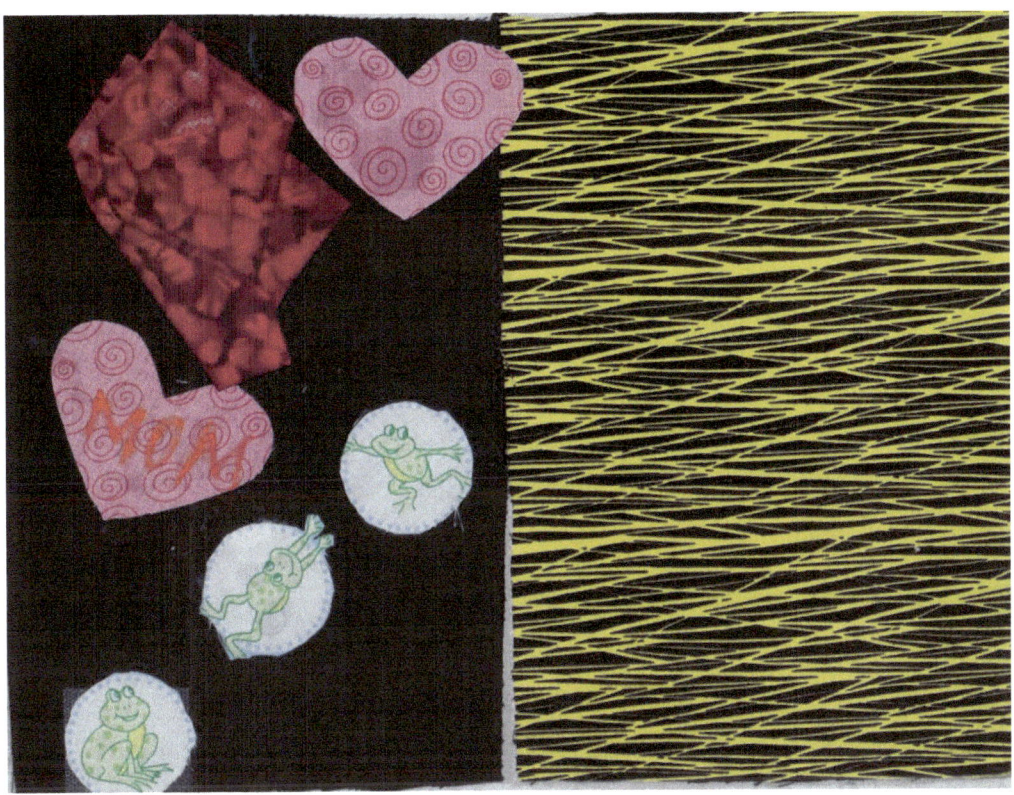

Jenci, age 13

Jenci spoke about his transition while living in the shelter. When he moved with his mother, brother and two sisters, he "felt very sad because [he] was homeless and then [he] arrived in the recreation program. [They] danced and that cheered [him] up."

In his piece, the yellow and black side represents the anger he felt when he first arrived at the shelter. The other side has a dark blue background and jumping frogs to show how he is making friends at the recreation program and "leaping to success." And finally, the hearts and flower show the love that he has for his mother.

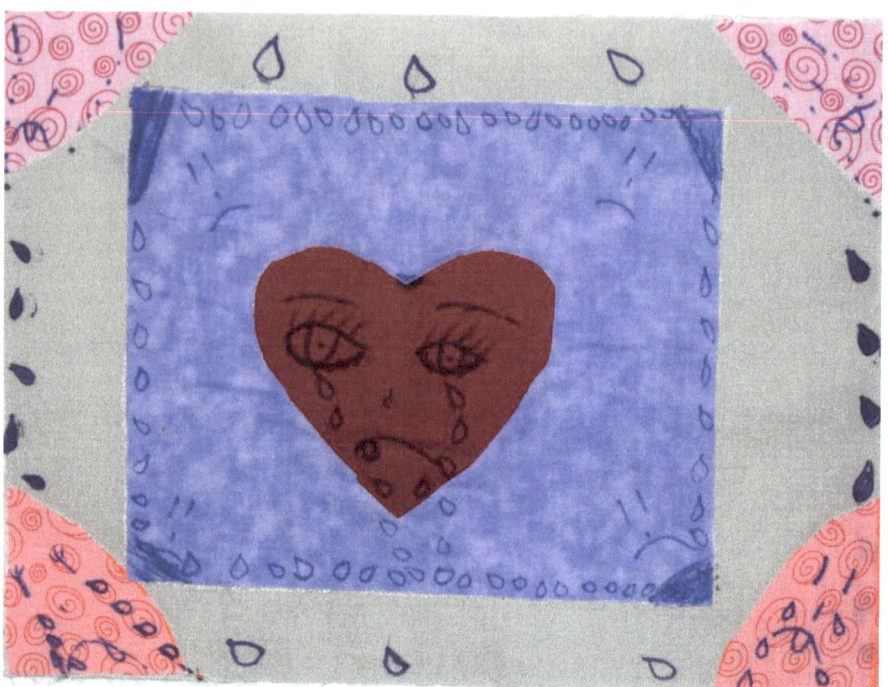

Yamilet, age 10, lives with her mother, brothers, and baby sister. She said that she sometimes feels sad and down because they don't have their own home. In her piece, she used red, purple and pink because those colors make her think of sad moments.

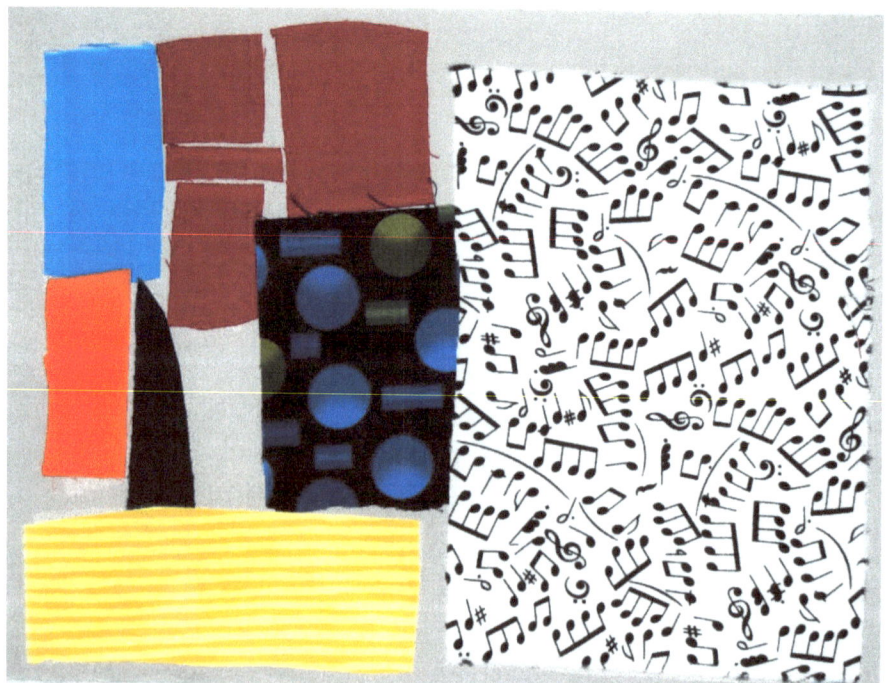

Cristian, age 11 has been living in the shelter with his father for 3 years. He likes living in the shelter because it's clean and warm. Before they moved in, it was very cold, he couldn't play and he "thought [he] was going to die." In the piece, each color represents a different feeling from before and after moving into the shelter.

BELT SHELTER
QUEENS, NY

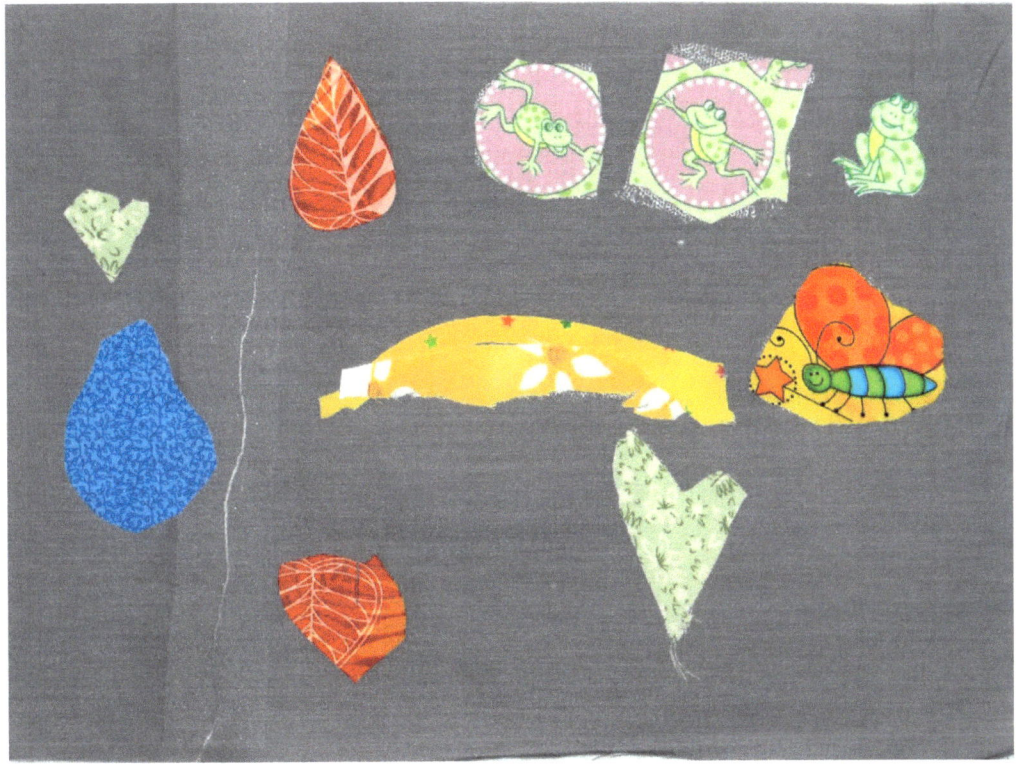

Justice, age 11

Justice feels "sad" living in the shelter with her mother and sister. She said being homeless is "hard because I lost my grandmother and we had little money so we could barely eat."

In her piece, each color and shape has meaning. The blue teardrop shows her sadness, the green heart shows that she is loved and the broken orange heart represents the people who don't like them because they don't have a home of their own.

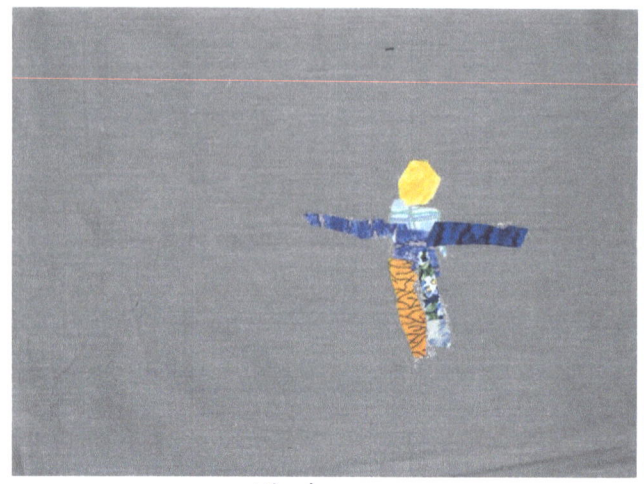

Nigel, age 7

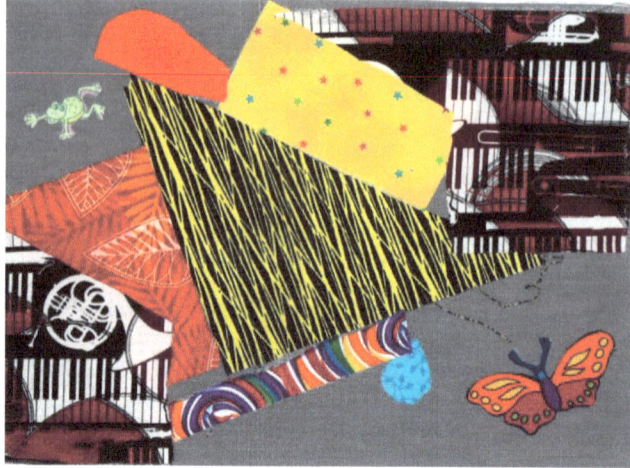

Tayray, age 11

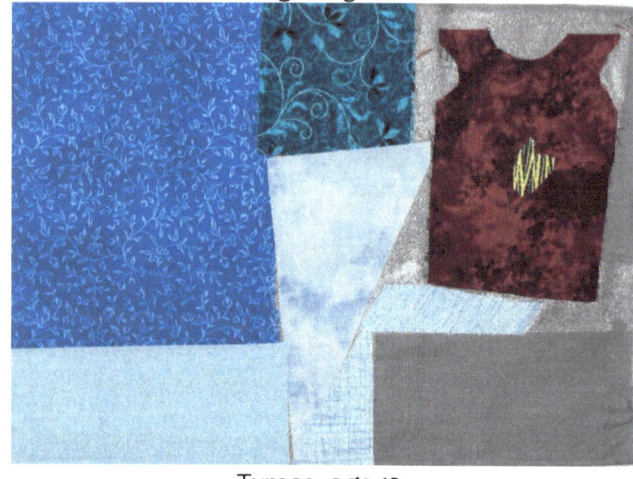

Tyrese, age 12

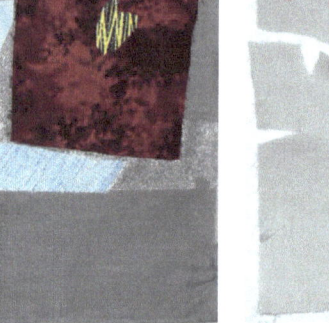

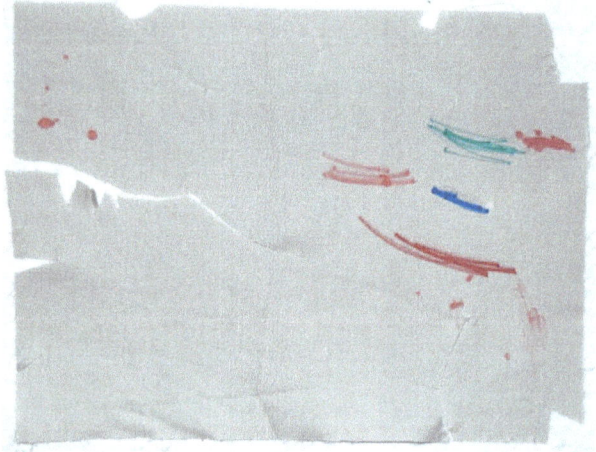

Anonymous, age 4

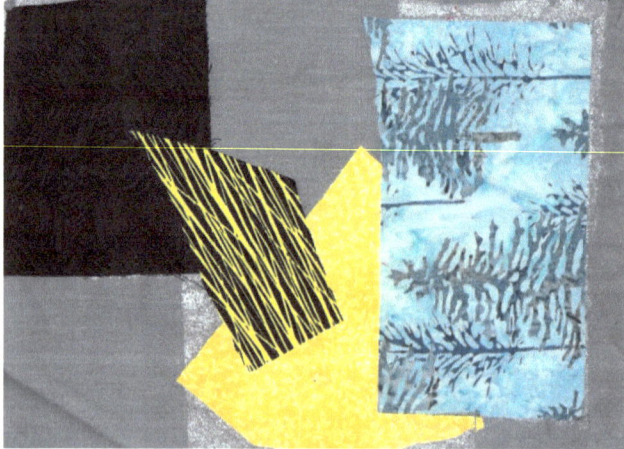

Jamilya, age 9

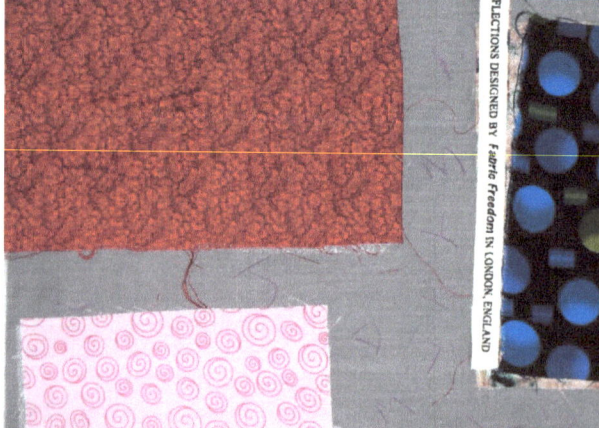

Joy, age 8

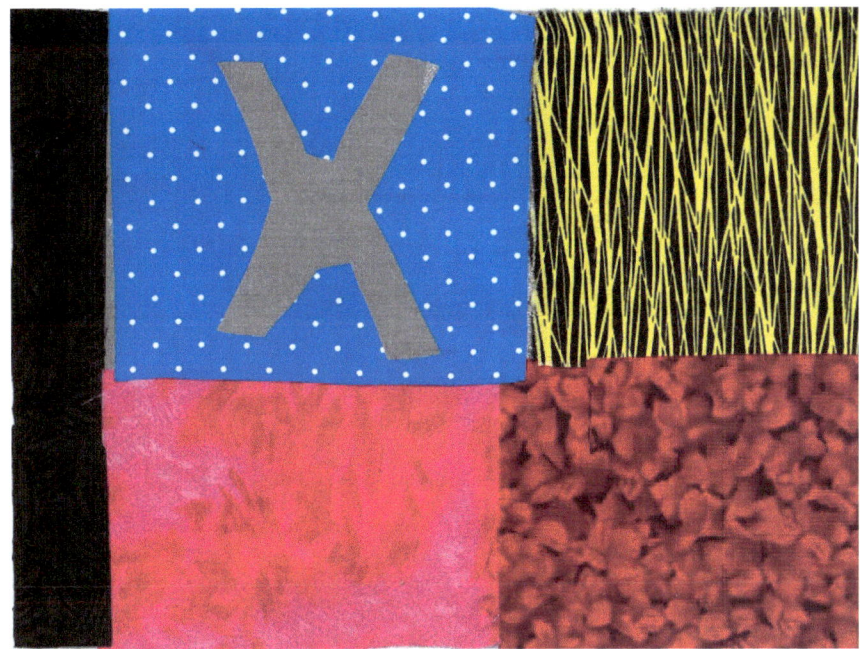

Kiana, age 11 said that when she first came to the shelter with her mother and aunt, she was "nervous, sad and angry." Now, however, "it feels good to be in the shelter." The left and top of her piece capture her feelings of anger and sadness when she first arrived at the shelter and the bottom shows her happiness.

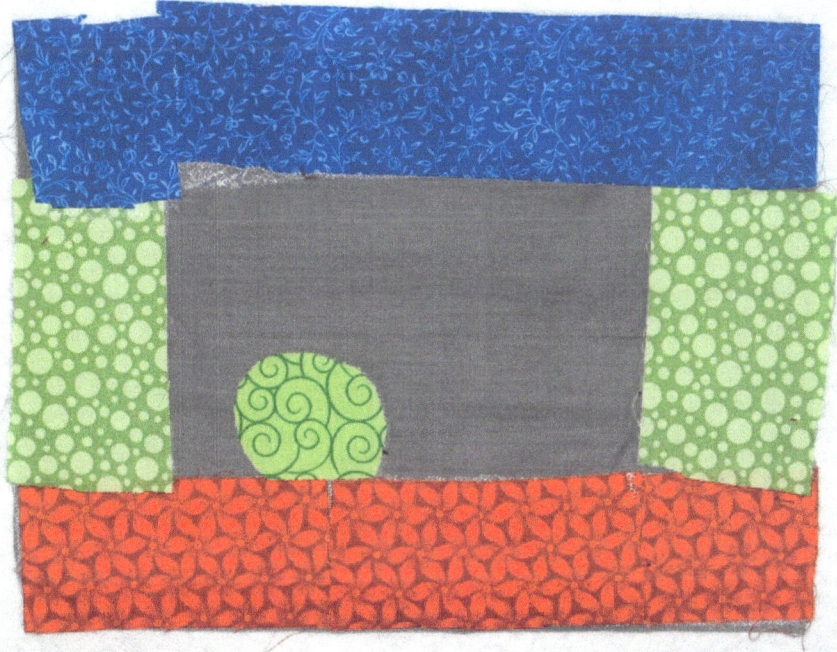

Andrew, age 9, lives in the shelter with his father. Each color in his piece represents a different feeling. The blue is his sadness, orange shows his happiness, and the green represents his anger.

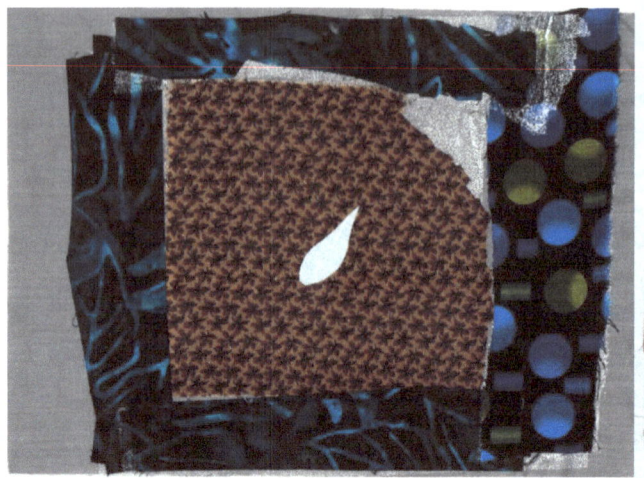

Patricia, age 7

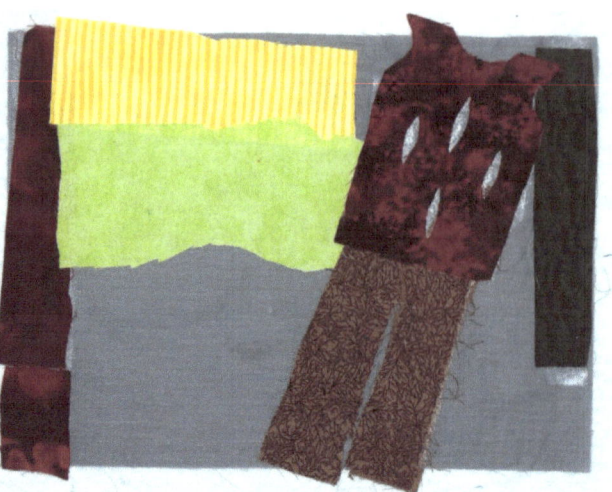

Nichelle, age 14

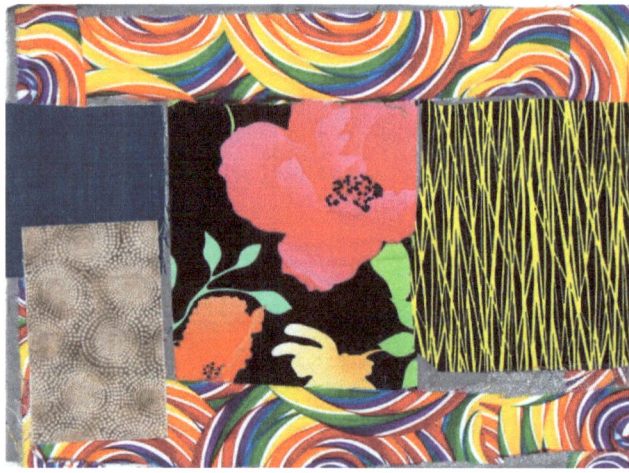

Jamiah, age 8

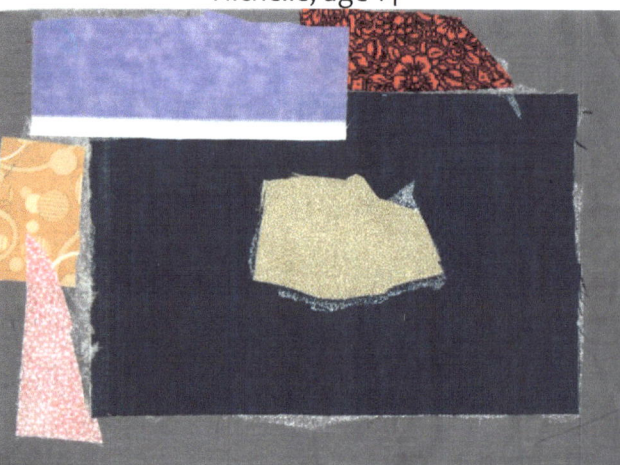

Kutar, age 9

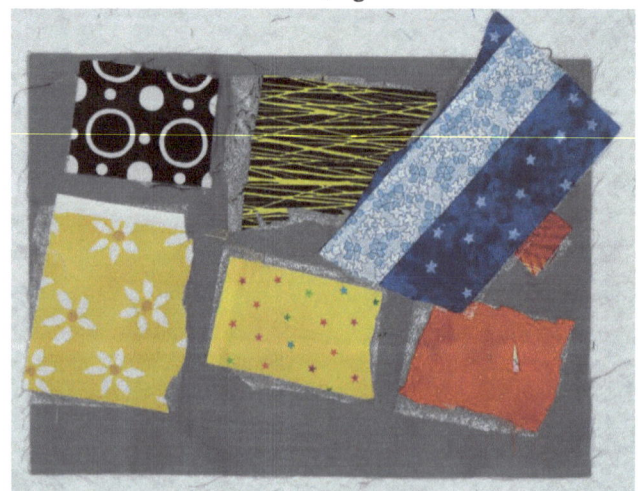

Christian, age 11

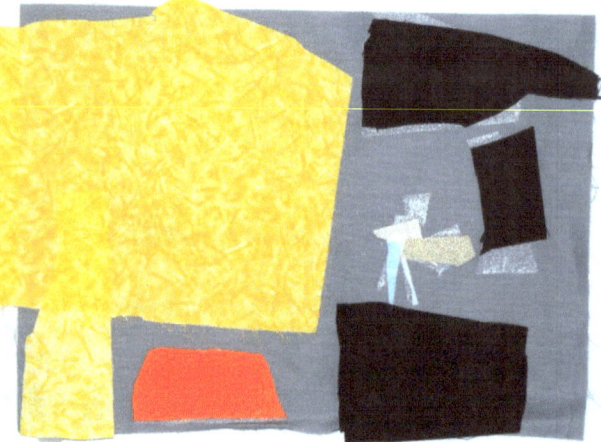

Nigel, age 7

PHIPPS TOWN AND COUNTRY RESIDENCE
BRONX, NEW YORK

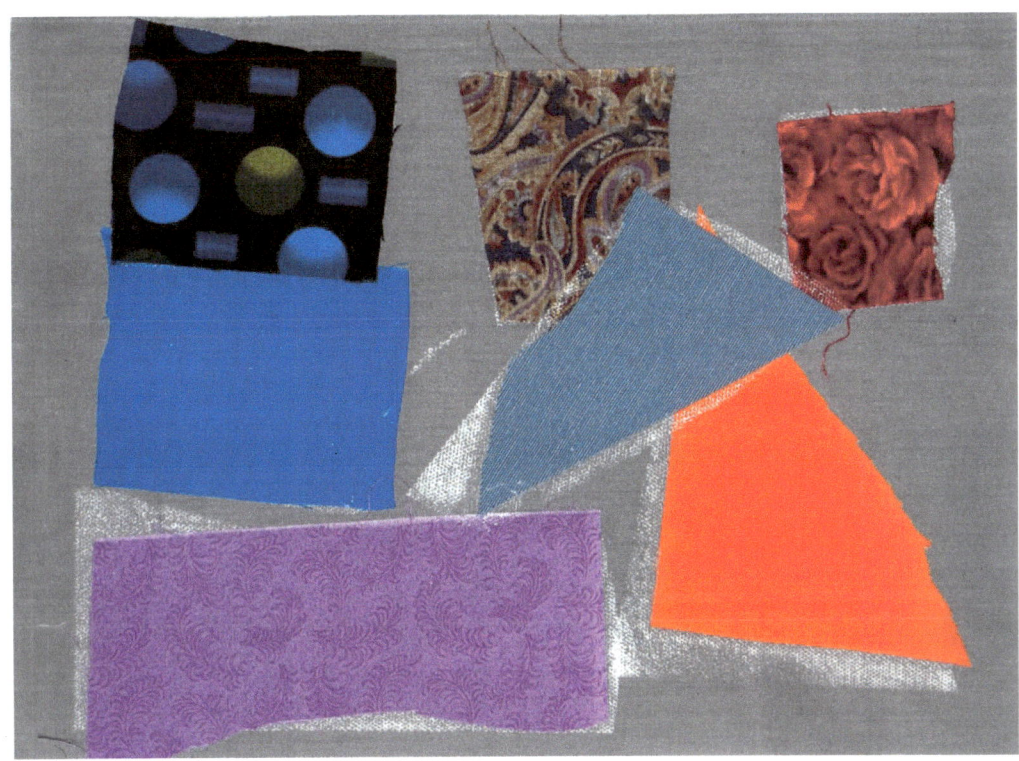

Taijani, age 11

Taijani lives in the shelter with her mother. When she first moved in, she "felt sad and scared." Her mother told her to "calm down and be happy" and she was able to take this advice once she saw her room and it felt more like home.

In her piece, each fabric represents a different emotion she has felt living at the shelter. The black fabric with purple circles shows her happiness, the blue represents sadness, the light purple is for her boredom, the light blue shows sleepiness, the paisley print is depression, and orange and red are for anger.

Kevan, age 7, has been in the shelter with his mother for 8 months. He said that living in the shelter is "great" because he likes the afterschool program.

It makes him happy to come to the program after school and he created his piece with his happy colors – green and blue.

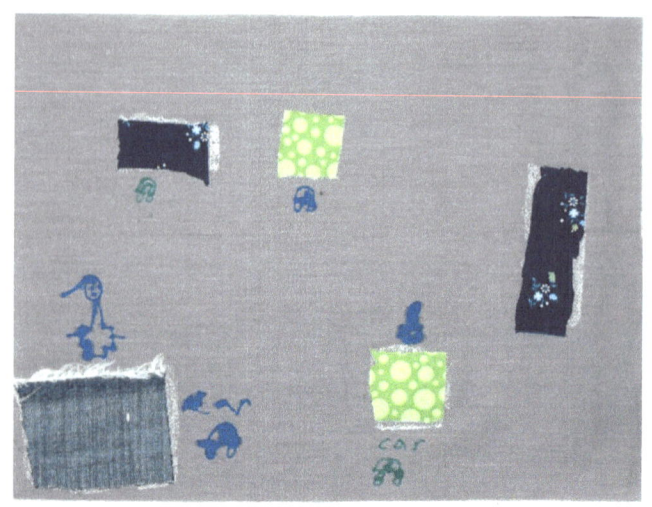

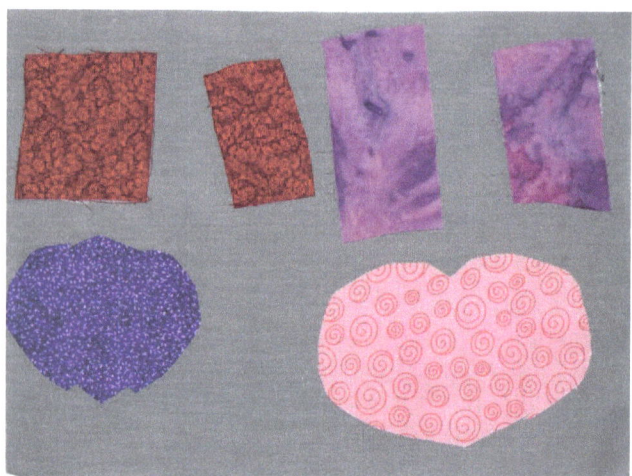

Kalisha, age 8, lives in the shelter with her mother and brother. She said that she is "happy being here" even though it's a little noisy and she sometimes feels lonely.

Her piece uses her happy colors – red, purple and pink.

Kaysha, age 7, doesn't like living in the shelter with her mother. She misses her old house where the park was open all the time and she had friends in her old school. She said that she feels "sad and lonely."

Each color in her piece represents a different emotion. Brown and black represent sadness, red is for anger, green shows loneliness, and orange shows the beginning of compromise as she and her mother settle into this new life.

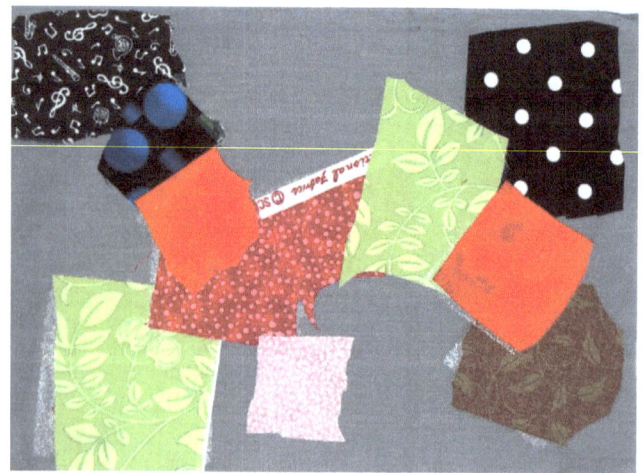

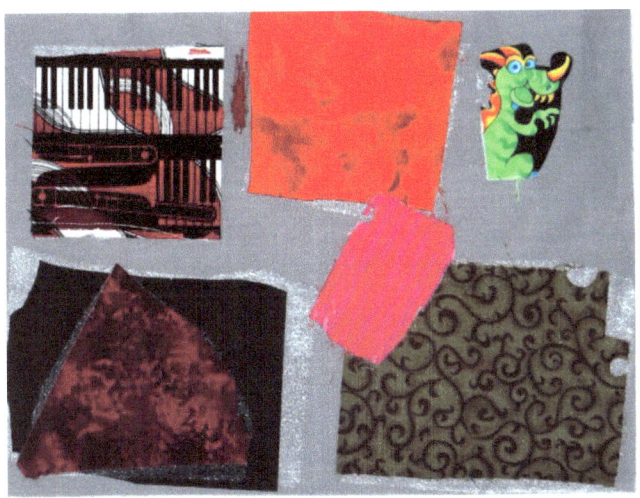

Jada, age 6

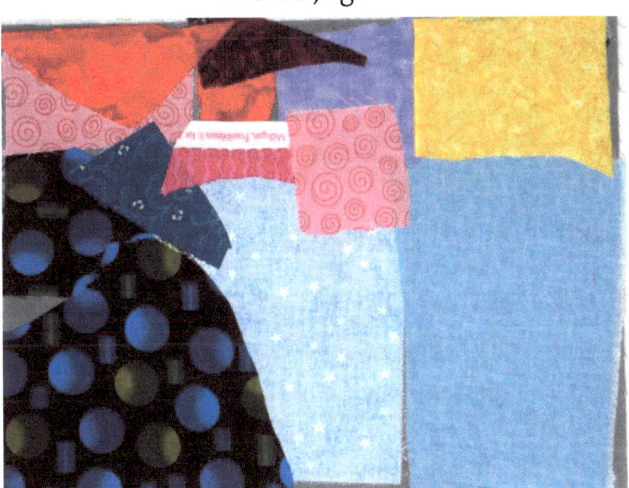

Michael, age 10

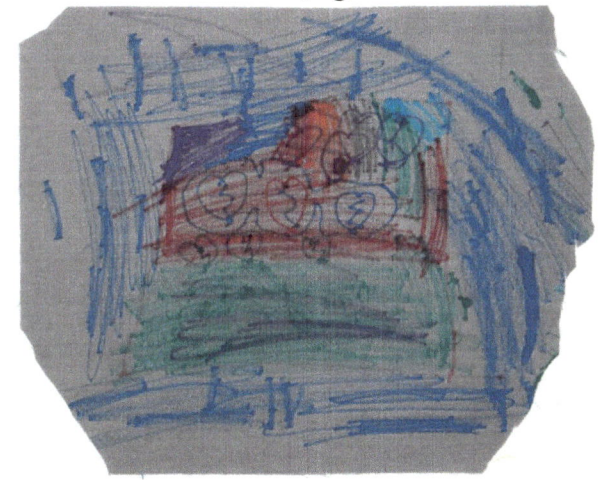

Allinson, age 6

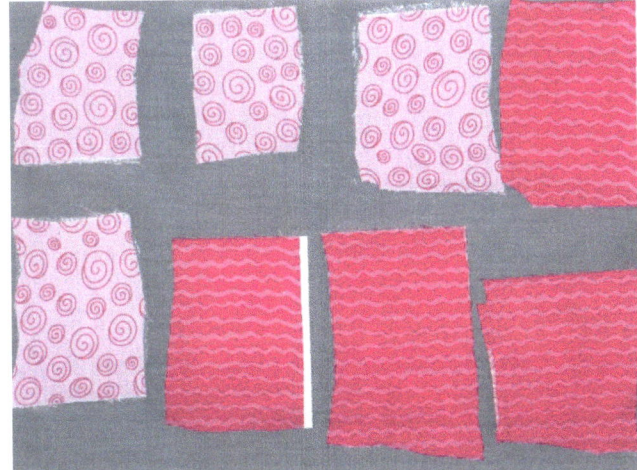
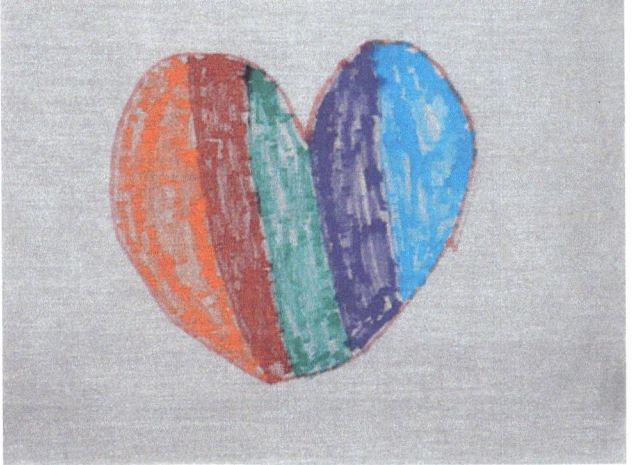

Kalisha, age 8

SCO SHELTER
BRONX, NY

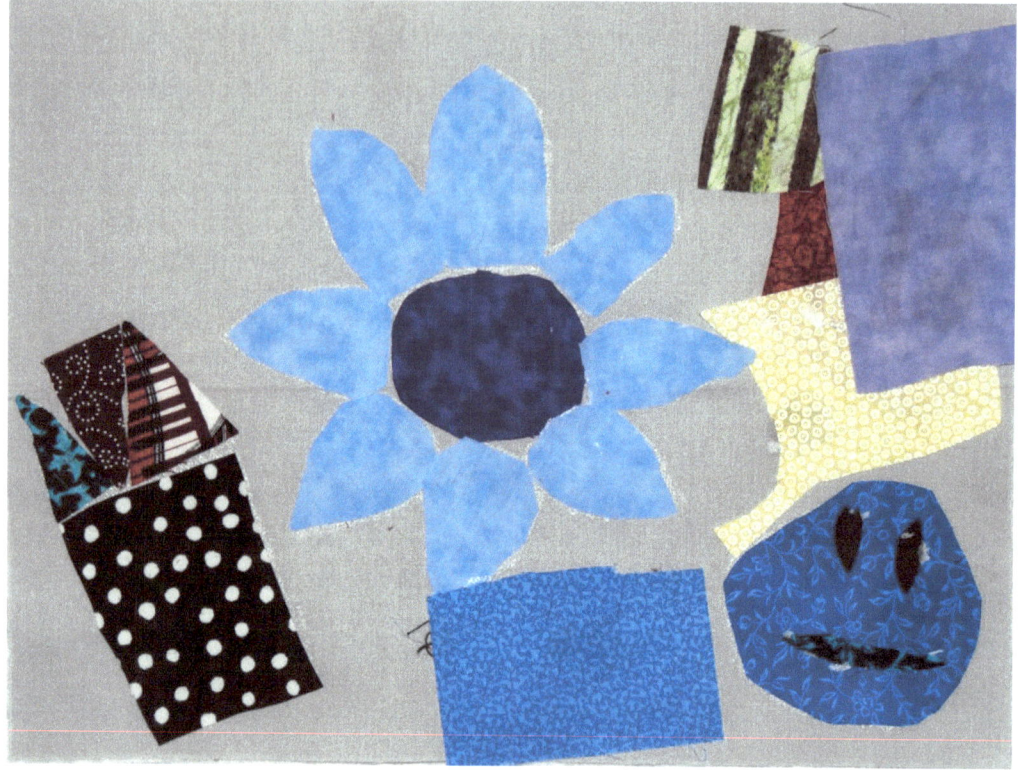

Kimone, age 12

Kimone, who lives with her mother, thinks that living in the shelter is fun. She said, "If there was no shelter, we would be on the streets."

The colors and shapes in her piece show the happiness and thankfulness she feels for the shelter.

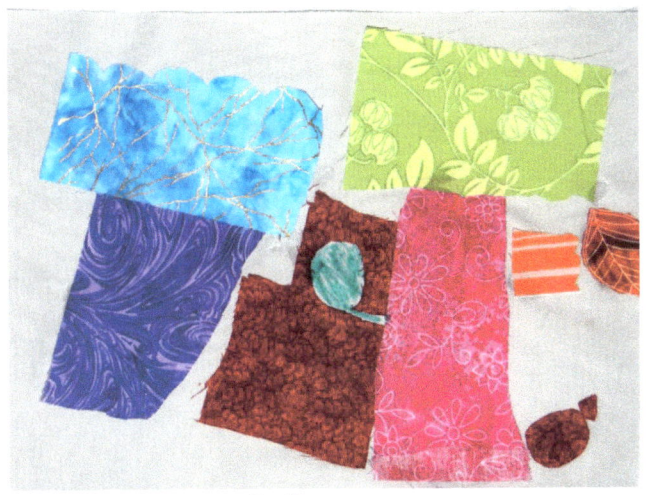

Emily, age 5

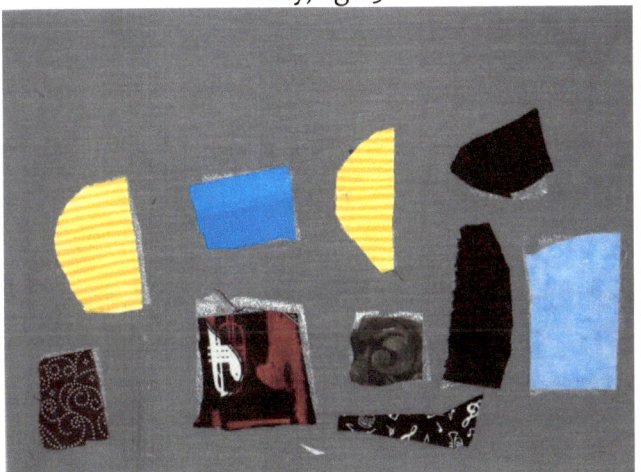

Pedro, age 7

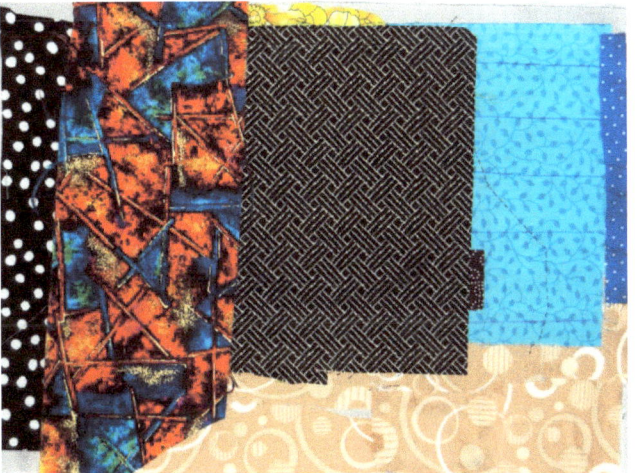

Jahamichah, age 8

Devonna, age 8

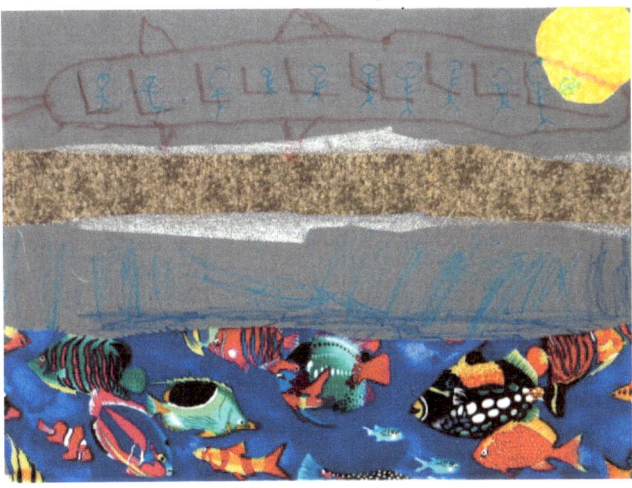

Aiyana, age 7

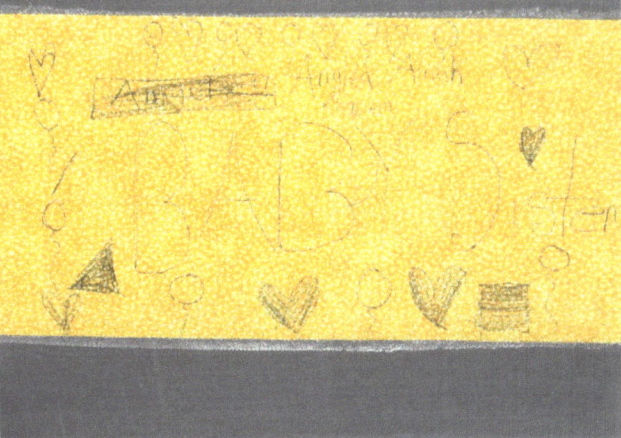

Khasiem, age 8

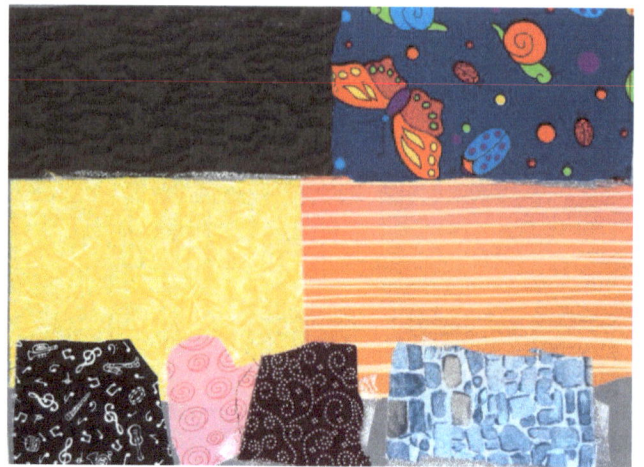

Jaden, age 11, feels that living in the shelter is "just like any other place." He made his piece about the excitement he felt when he went on a trip to a basketball game with the recreation program.

The colors yellow, orange, green and pink represent his happiness and excitement.

Kemenah, age 9, has been living in the shelter for 7 months with her mother and two brothers. She was sad to leave her friends when she had to move, but made many new friends at the shelter.

She made her piece with colors and shapes that make her happy.

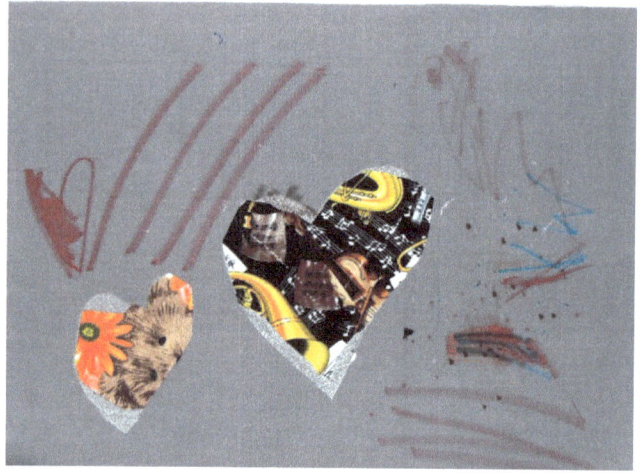

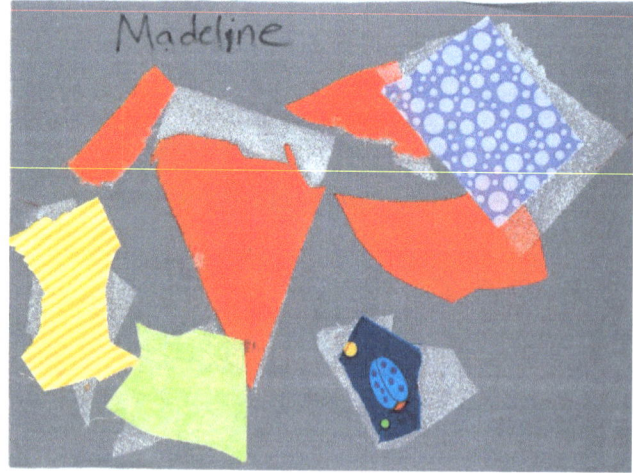
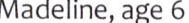

Madeline, age 6

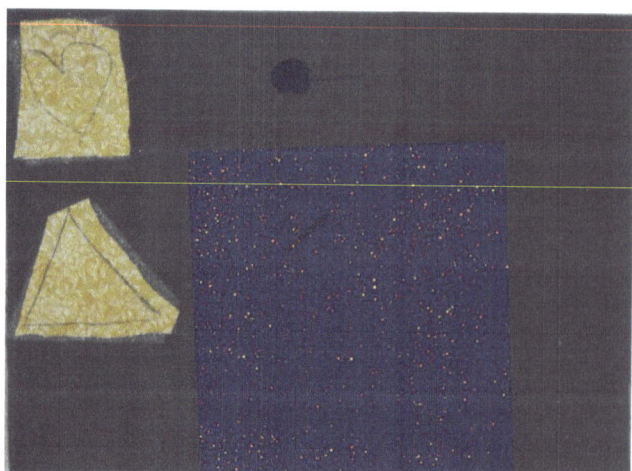

Mahagani, age 6

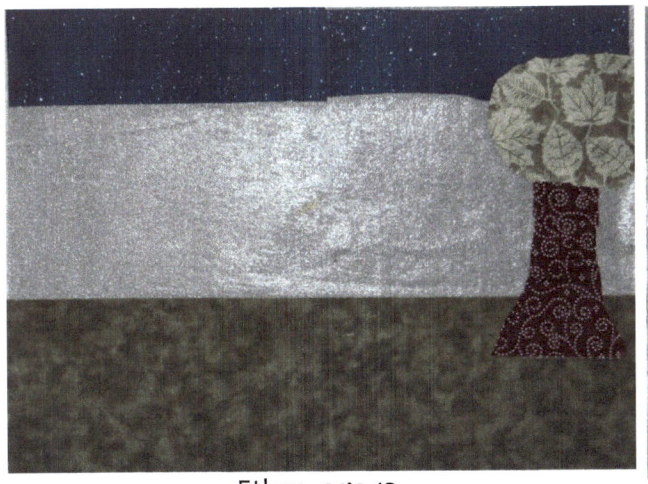

Ethan, age 13

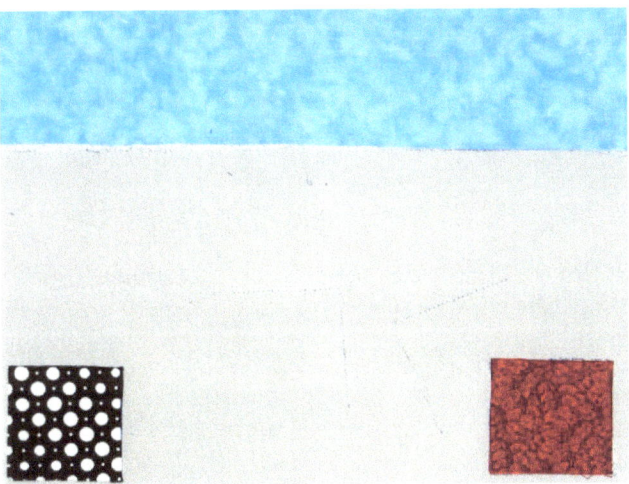

Dasia, age 6

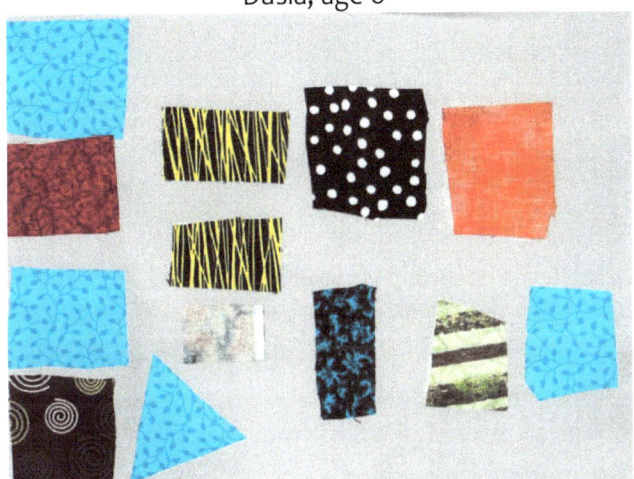

Terell, age 13

Jamar, age 13

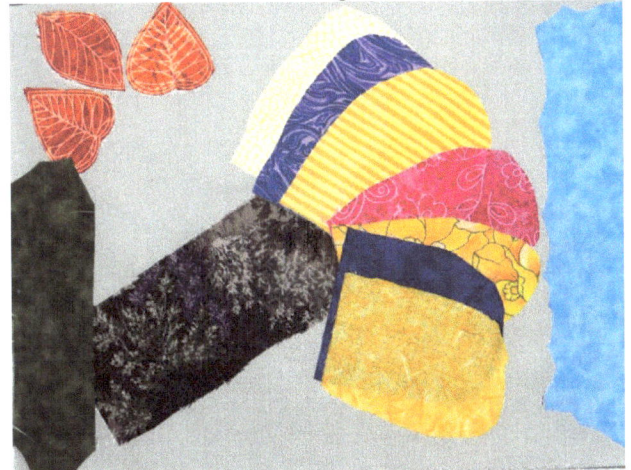

Chioma, SCO Volunteer (age 17)

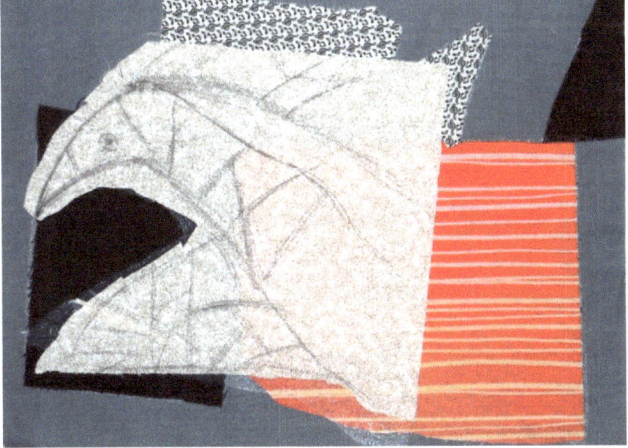

Brandon, SCO Volunteer (age 14)

TILDEN HALL
BROOKLYN, NY

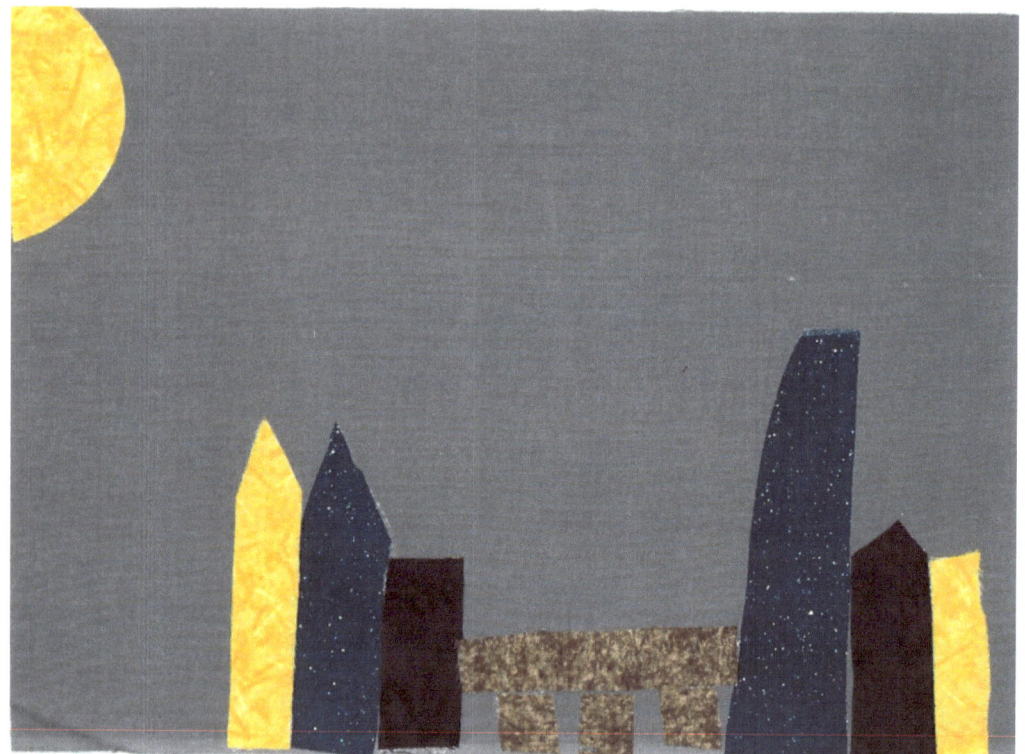

Alex, age 14

Alex moved from Florida to Tilden Hall three months ago with his mother, brother, and two sisters. He said, "It is a stressful life living in the shelter. My life being homeless is full of journeys and traveling and sleeping in hotels." Through all these journeys, he has felt both happy and sad.

For this piece, he decided to focus on his happy feelings, represented by joyful colors: blue, purple and yellow. These colors are used in his piece to create a city scene with a bridge to show that he is happy in his new city.

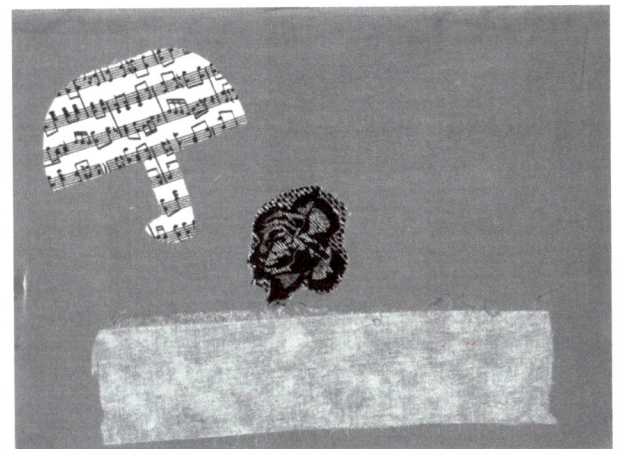
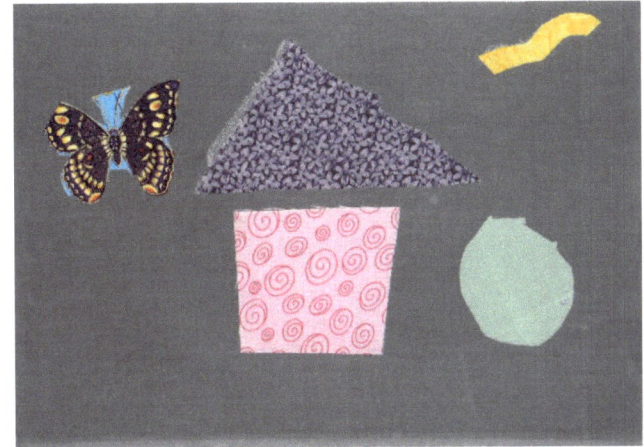

LaShaye, age 5

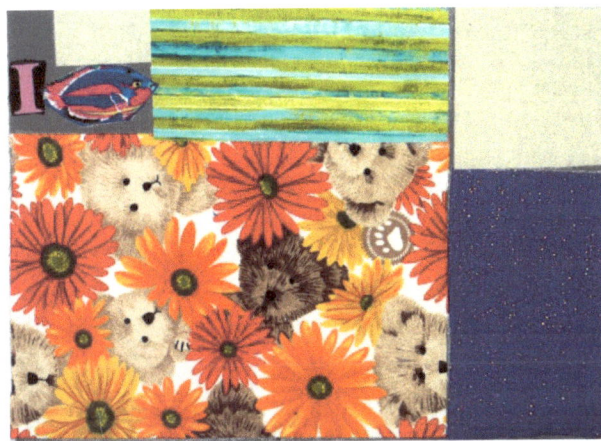

Ines, age 11

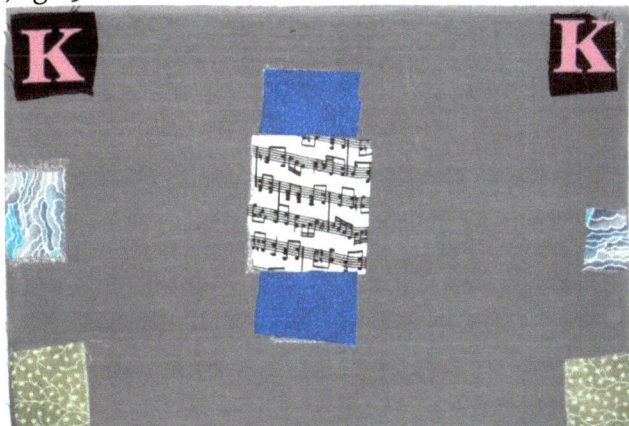

David, age 7

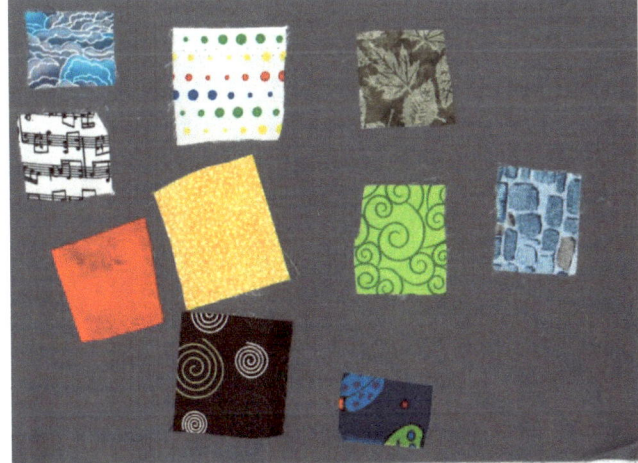

Travon, age 12

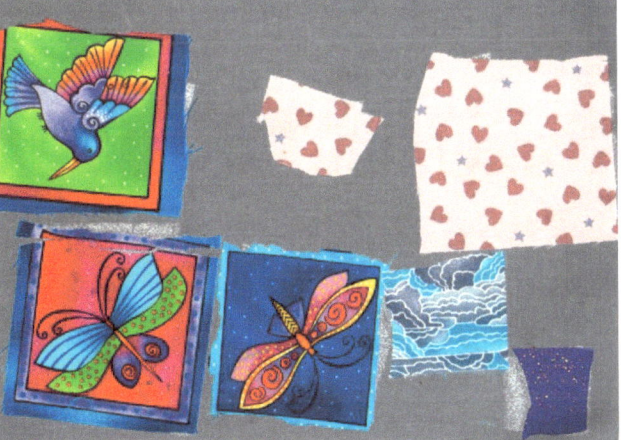

Jacerra, age 8

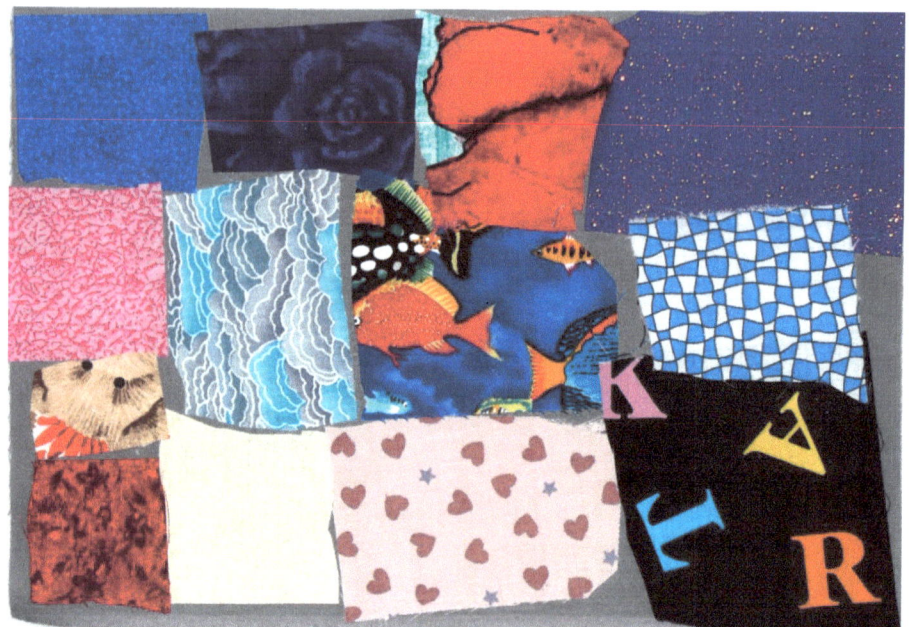

Taynayishia, age 9, likes living with her mother and three brothers, but is sad that they are in a shelter. She chose to use sad colors in her piece: blue, green, red and pink.

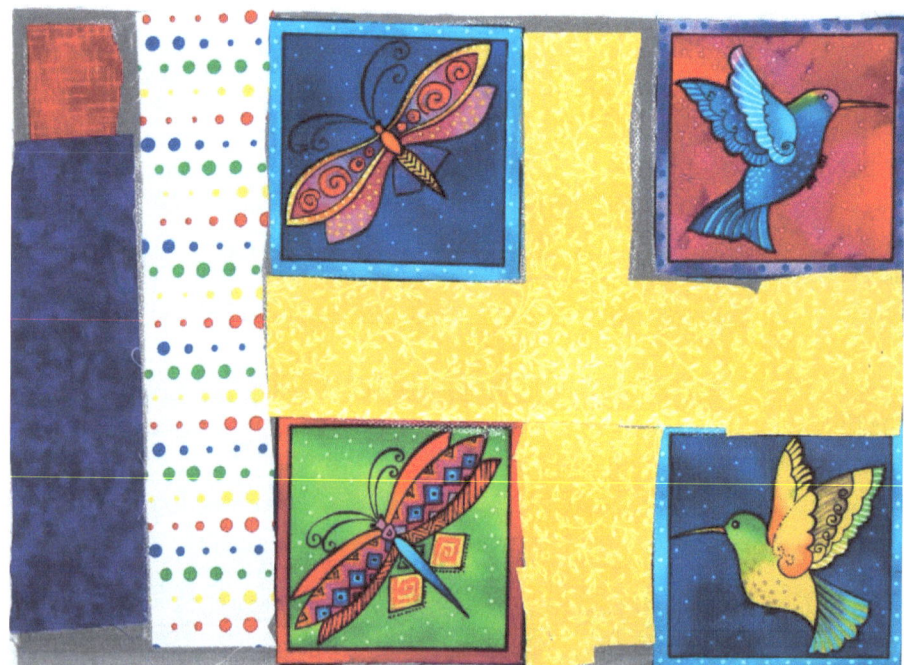

Janacia, age 11 moved to the shelter a year ago with her mother and sister. She said that she hates living in a shelter, but tries not to think about it. To acknowledge the hatred, she put a small red square in the top left corner, but made the rest of her piece cheerful.

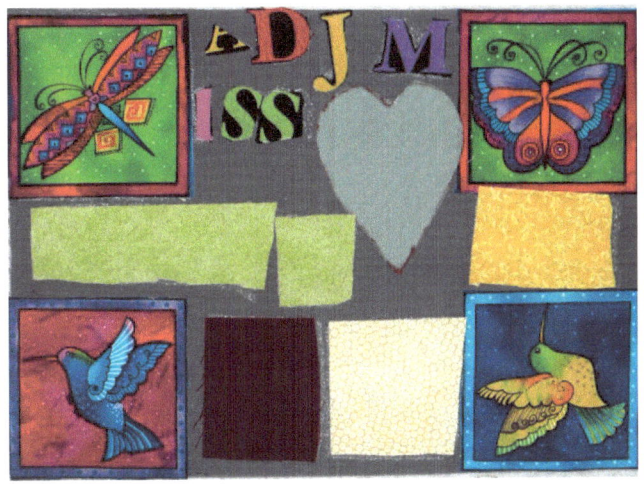

Hadja, age 11

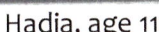

Johany, age 6

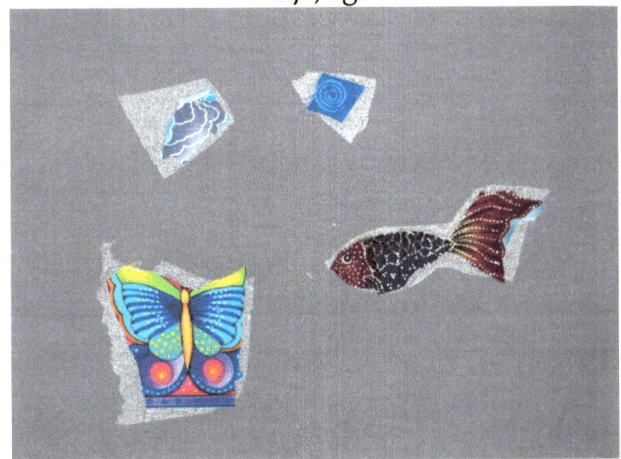

Andres, age 7

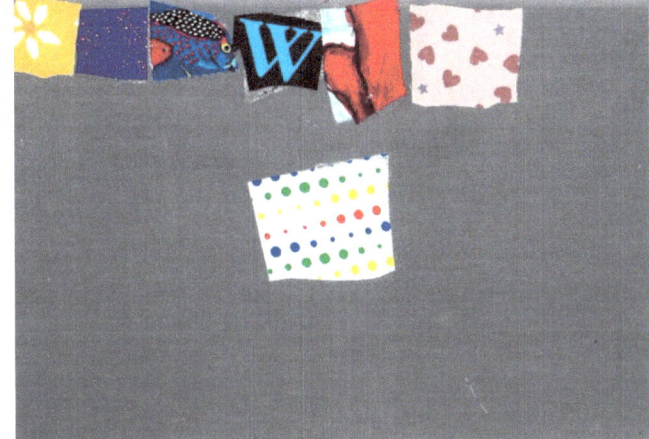

Wendy, age 7

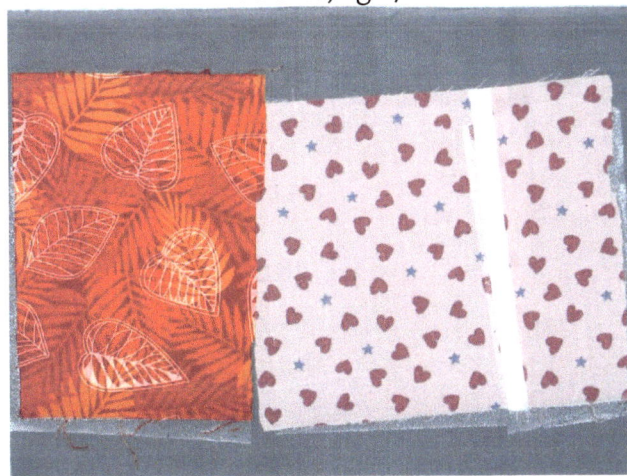

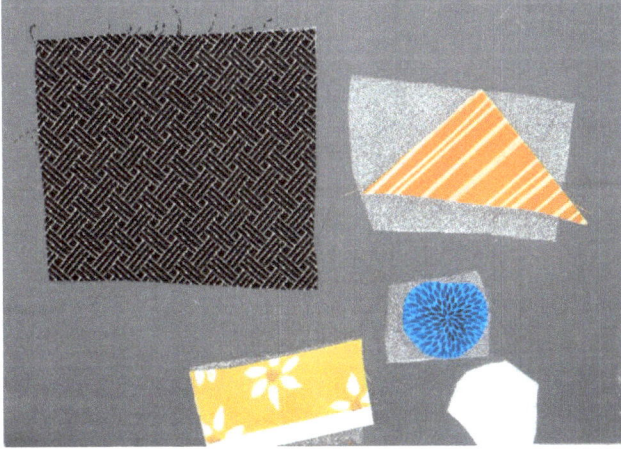

Nadia, age 6

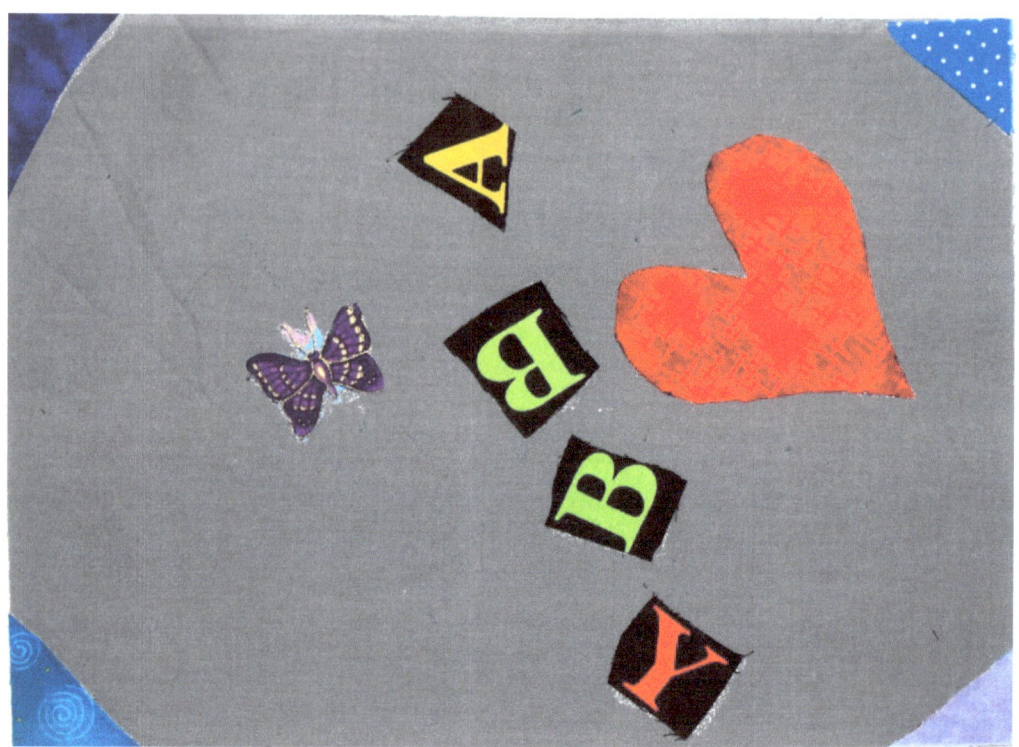

Abigail, age 12

Abigail moved from foster care to life in the shelter with her father. She said living in the shelter is just like life anywhere else. "The only difference is that we are humans who need help."

ABOUT THE ARTIST

Heather G. Stoltz is a fiber artist with an MA in Jewish Women's Studies from the Jewish Theological Seminary of America and a BA in Jewish Studies and BS in Mechanical Engineering from Lafayette College. Her quilted wall hangings feature themes from classic Jewish texts and social justice issues.

Stoltz is the co-president of the Women's Caucus for Art New York Chapter, and her work has been exhibited at many venues including the Park Avenue Synagogue in NYC and JOFA's 10th Anniversary International Conference. She was an Arts Fellow at the Drisha Institute from 2008-2010 and was an Artist-in Residence for the National Havurah Committee in the summer of 2008, where she taught the class "Translating Text into Textile." Her work has also been featured in *Jewish Threads: A Hands-On Guide to Stitching Spiritual Intention into Jewish Fabric Crafts, Creative Quilting: The Journal Quilt Project* and *Zeek Magazine.*

She lives in New York City with her husband, Geoff Mitelman, who is a rabbi and writer.

To see more of Stoltz's work, visit her website at http://sewingstories.com.

www.ingramcontent.com/pod-product-compliance
Lightning Source LLC
Chambersburg PA
CBHW051045180526
45172CB00002B/522